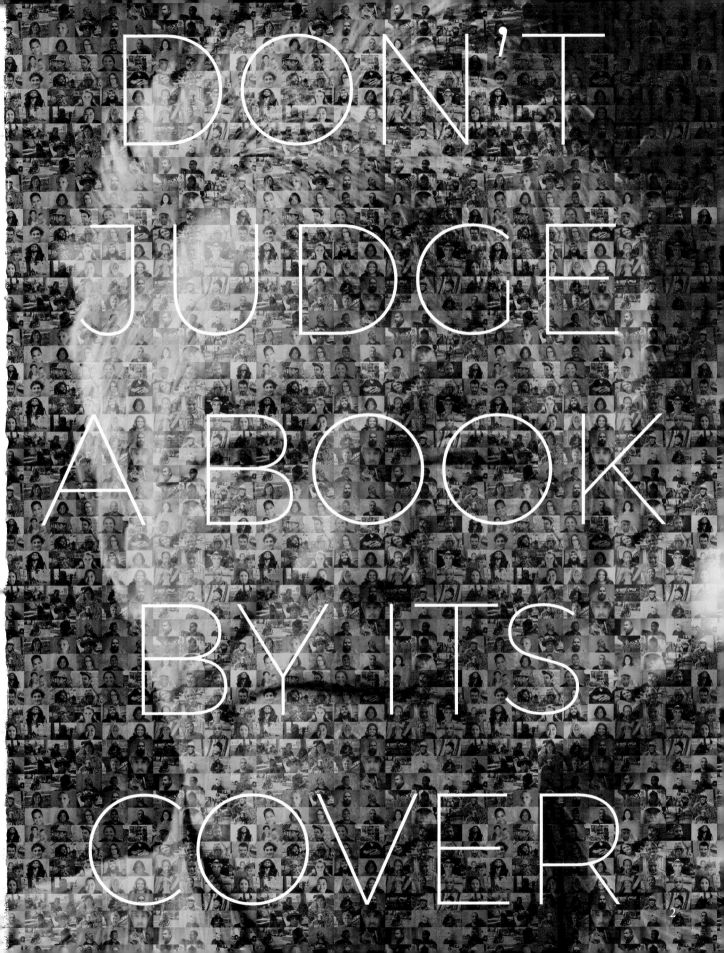

DON'T JUDGE A BOOK BY ITS COVER

Fifty Sandwiches is a 501(c)3 nonprofit project dedicated to raising awareness and taking steps to solve our nation's homeless crisis.

In honor of all the men, women, and children experiencing homelessness he's met on his Fifty Sandwiches journey, author Justin Doering is making a gift to the Salvation Army with a portion of the proceeds from his book. Remaining funds are directed back to Fifty Sandwiches for future endeavors.

To learn more, see page 120 or go to FiftySandwiches.com.

An estimated 3.5 million people experience homelessness in this country annually.[40]

Who are these people?

Statistics don't answer that question. Numbers on a sheet don't leave us with the emotional investment to see homeless people for the individuals they are.

Homelessness is an aspect of the human experience that is often overlooked and profiled by the general public. The issue of homelessness is too often dehumanized into statistics and considered an inevitable consequence of the social food chain.

However, when put front and center, their experiences and struggles lend light to our natural desire to parallel the lives of others with our own. In other words, voices and faces speak louder than statistics.

A SPECIAL THANKS TO:

● ●

My parents, Donal and Sandy Doering: *for their lifelong love and support, and for exemplifying the selfless ambition needed to create this project in the first place.*

Camden Doering: *for his volunteer research work in the project and his commitment to better the lives of others.*

Rolan Marie Yetter: *for his thoughtful critique and endless adherence to both the project and myself.*

Ryan Glasky and the Glasky family: *for acting as a second family and for their inherent empathy for the lives of others.*

Erica Chappell: *for being the most ambitious and helpful intern anyone can ask for.*

The 50 individuals that follow: *for their companionate divulgence of unfiltered afflictions and perspectives made in their selfless effort to humanize the homeless.*

TABLE OF CONTENTS

• •

FIFTY SANDWICHES BACKERS

On May 15, 2016, 135 amazing people came together to fund a project to better understand the homeless experience in the United States. Their generosity, constant support, and desire to live in a more altruistic society brought Fifty Sandwiches to life.

● ●

Ace Edmonds
Alessandra Cristina & Ferreira Porto
Alli Nilges
Amy & Chris Hoover
Aswin Ramakrishnan
Austin Ward
Ben
Beth Clarke
Betta Games
Bill Schilz
Bob Arnold
Brandon Reagan
Brenda & Bruce Howard
Brendan Bell-Taylor
Brent Little
Brian Loper
Bryan Bachterajaya
Byron Fabiano
Carol Gonzales
Carolyn Ridgway
Cem Bozkuş
Chiara Zuccarino-Crowe
Chris Breazeal
Chris Glasky
Christina Mcdaniels
Christine McComas
Christopher Chambers
Cindy Doss
Dale & Dawn Crabb
Dave
David Eisenberg

David Hunsaker
David K Lee
Derick Hildebrandt
Derik Ellis
Devon Loy
Diane Rosenblum
Donal Doering
Donald Watts
Elizabeth Mccloy
Erica Gentry Hammond
Gabriel Martin
Goodnight Question
Greg Nilges
Gretchen Anderson
Grub Hub Camp Kitchens
Gustaf Bjorklund
Hailey Doss
Hannah Simmons
Holly Stubbs
Jackie Carlson
James Goodrich
Jarrett Johnson
Jaicie Yetter
Jason Raymond
Jen Kline Clark
Jenny Doering
Jesse
Jim Doering
Joan Phillips
Jonathan Khoo
Jordan

Josh Crockett & Kristin **Slaysman**

Jules

Julie Groff

Julie Yetter

Justin Erickson

Kaitlyn

Karen Cadle

Karthik Hemmanur

Katherine Stafford Butler

Kayla Spooner

Kayla Strand

Keith Carpenter

Kenna Yetter

Kevin Glasky

Kim Borsheim

Kirwin Webb

Kristin Mcdonald

Kyle Gormley

Kyle Yetter

Laura King

Laura Lande

Laura Rose Bull

Linda Riley

Lisa Burns

Lisa Fournier

Lisa Gardner

Lisa Troxel

Maggie

Maria

Maria Scott

Marion Elizabeth

Mark Grimes

Mark Satuloff

Martha Legare

Maureen

Michael Greene

Michelle Geil

Mike & Robyn McDonald

Mitch

Nancy Collins

Natacha Springer

Necdet Yücel

Peggy & Alan Wasserman

Plum Geek

R. Currey

Rebecca Perry

Rens Groothuijsen

Robert Hugh

Roger Herzler

Rolan Yetter

Roman Koshlyak

Ryan Glasky

Sandy Doering

Sara Colbert

Sara Senger

Sean Palmer

Simon Yanni

Stacia Andrews

Stephanie Law

Stephanie Tice

Stewart Kilgore

Sune Bøegh

Susan & Dave Muscarella

Sydney Williams

Taran Loper

The Millennial Academy

Thomas

Tiana Pierce

Tim Atwell

Tobias

Trica Yetter

Tyler

Vien

Wow Youza

Zarroc

A B O U T

The Mission

Fifty Sandwiches is a nonprofit project dedicated to presenting the public with a rare glimpse into the lives and experiences of America's homeless. With a goal to close the gap between public perception and reality, Fifty Sandwiches aims to foster the realization that there is more to homelessness than being homeless by creating an emotional bridge between readers and the struggling strangers they walk past every day.

The Plan

STEP 1

Spread the word of Fifty Sandwiches and fund the project via Kickstarter.

STEP 2

Circumnavigate the country documenting the stories and faces behind America's homeless by offering sandwiches in exchange for interviews.

STEP 3

Cram the stories into a book, using personal accounts of those who are homeless to encourage public awareness and understanding.

The Journey

After purchasing Milo, my 1990 GMC Vandura for the hefty sum of $1,200, I embarked on my three-and-a-half-month journey throughout the United States. Coasting at a cool 13 mpg, I sought sleep in Walmart parking lots, street corners, and state parks. Armed with a camera and a recorder, I reached out to homeless shelters and programs throughout the nation, splitting my interviews between shelters and people I approached on the street.

THE ROUTE

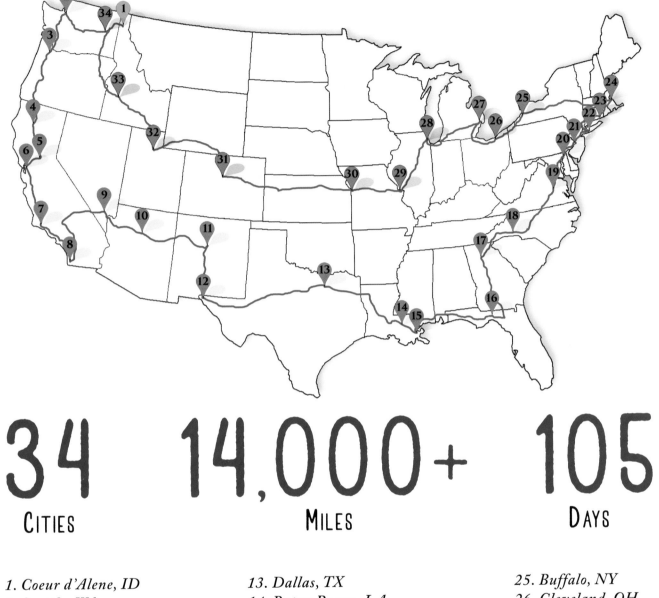

34
CITIES

14,000+
MILES

105
DAYS

1. Coeur d'Alene, ID
2. Seattle, WA
3. Portland, OR
4. Redding, CA
5. Sacramento, CA
6. San Francisco, CA
7. Los Angeles, CA
8. San Diego, CA
9. Las Vegas, NV
10. Flagstaff, AZ
11. Albuquerque, NM
12. El Paso, TX

13. Dallas, TX
14. Baton Rouge, LA
15. New Orleans, LA
16. Tallahassee, FL
17. Atlanta, GA
18. Charlotte, NC
19. Richmond, VA
20. Washington D.C., BC
21. Philadelphia, PA
22. New York, NY
23. Norwalk, CT
24. Boston, MA

25. Buffalo, NY
26. Cleveland, OH
27. Detroit, MI
28. Chicago, IL
29. Saint Louis, MO
30. Kansas City, MO
31. Denver, CO
32. Salt Lake, UT
33. Boise, ID
34. Spokane, WA

From the Atlantic to the Pacific, from the Mexican border to the Canadian border, Milo's journey is depicted throughout its circumnavigation of the United States.

THE INTERVIEWS

The interviews were informal, intimate discussions lasting anywhere from half an hour to three hours. Each chat evolved into a dynamic collection of life struggles, stories, and philosophies from a population rarely given a voice. Upon departure, my only expectation was to have no expectations, yet somehow, I often found myself bewildered. Each interview revealed a new shade of light to the spectrum of homelessness, showing me a color I had not seen before. Each story served as a bittersweet reminder that I had little to no grasp on the sheer depth of this issue that I had thought myself to be well understood.

I quickly realized my mission outlined in the Kickstarter to capture a collective face to homelessness would require 500,000+ interviews.[1] Each interaction was far too distinct from one another to categorize as an entire subset of the population. While each story aims to humanize the homeless through emotional connection, the compilation of individual experiences now serves as a testament to the sheer diversity of the homeless population.

These are stories that want to be told and need to be heard.

• •

A societal crisis cannot be solved without first being understood.

The profiles that follow are true stories and experiences from the United States' most unknown, unwanted, and unheard.

• •

CANDACE, 38
COEUR D'ALENE, ID

"I had a great job and gradually fell behind on bills after my car broke down. I got stuck with payday loans, and it became an awful mess. We moved in with my sister and took over her lease but had to move out when I found out about some horrible things that had happened there soon after. We couch surfed from friend to friend trying to get back on track until we wore out our welcome."

"**Without a stable living environment, I felt like a failure, like I had failed my children.**"

"Everybody thinks that homelessness means you're sleeping on the street or your car. We're lucky it didn't come to that, but we still were living without stable housing. Having to pack your up your stuff every single day to move to a new place the next night was incredibly stressful with three children. My daughter was even bullied at school for not having a stable living environment."

"Eventually, I heard about Family Promise, and they took us in and helped us get back on our feet. Since then. we've just had a series of blessings. I started my own cleaning company last May, and it's been growing since then. I get to spend more time with my kids. I struggled to take care of my children financially. I would have to miss out on important things in their lives to make sure we had food. Without a stable living situation, I felt like a failure, like I had failed my children. I couldn't provide for them."

Children living with a lack of stable housing has been shown to lead to problems with physical health, developmental delays, emotional well-being, and academic underachievement. [58]

"Before we lost our apartment, I had unhealthy spending habits and was an emotional wreck. It's crazy to think that I make less money now and spend more on rent, but I'm feeling much better about myself. We overcame a lot. At some point, you have to make this choice. Am I going to let this defeat me? Or am I going to come out stronger? I chose to come out stronger. There were days when I would sit in my car and cry. We had amazing support from a lot of people though. God has always provided, just not always in the way that we anticipated.

After actually experiencing homelessness, my perspective has really grown. I feel like I used to play the victim, but now I'm able to look at things through a more positive lens. I used to think homeless people made poor choices, or do drugs, or drink. There are a lot more families than I had ever thought. We were judged to the point where you don't want to tell people that you don't have a place to stay. I didn't want to admit defeat. I would want someone to look at me in a positive light, and fearing judgement in the midst of everything we were going through made the experience a lot more terrifying. I've learned not to judge people just because they are facing more adversity than I. It can happen to anybody."

SCOOBY, 25
SEATTLE, WA

"I have been out here for seven years. I am out here by choice, and I am here to learn. People may see us doing the same thing every day, but it is unbelievable what I have learned from human nature out here. In many ways, talking to people can be compared to the knowledge you gain from reading a book. What I have failed to read, I have experienced in many cases. This is a learning experience for me. I like to think my experience can be a learning experience for others as well. I want to learn about people, and this is an excellent perspective to do that from.

The most outstanding lesson I have learned out here is to be thankful, and more importantly, to produce more in the universe to be thankful for. I want to be an ambassador of goodwill, a mercenary of faith for the people living on the streets. I'm a good person who is just here to learn, and I have met a lot of other good people who have taken the same path as me."

> **"This is a learning experience for me. I like to think my experience can be a learning experience for others as well."**

"When you're out here, people think you're a virus, but it's not to say that is undeserved because you have to protect yourself. People are going to shy away from strangers who seem intimidating, and I understand that. Protecting yourself and protecting your family is part of human nature and who am I to get offended by human nature?

I volunteer once a week with a group to clean the streets around this area. I do it to give back to the community a bit. There are times when people give me a meal or food, and I don't have anything to give in return but my service. I think it's essential to have a strong relationship with your community."

Seattle's homeless population nearly doubled in the just five years, rising from a 2012 estimate of 2,594 homeless people to the 2017 estimated count at 5,485.[18,44]

PEGGY, 59
PORTLAND, OR

"I've been living off and on the streets since I was 15. I left due to abuse from my mom and never looked back. I'm in temporary housing now, but I'd still be on the streets if I weren't living on disability. I'm living on less than 800 bucks a month, and after bills, I will have around fifty dollars leftover. I don't want to live under a bridge anymore. When I could walk, I could do it; I could swing the streets. Domestic violence is what forced me to live on the streets, and harassment and abuse are what forced me to find housing again.

For homeless women, housing is often such a tough choice. We're not women anymore when we're out there. People don't want to get their hands shook by me. However, they are always ready to give advice. I remember being told to 'Find a man in your life and they can take care of you and your kids.' I do that then suddenly they are spending too much time with the kids. He begins to like the kids and feel for them more than he likes you. The monster in him shows, and he gets taken away."

"I couldn't get out of the house when I was going through domestic abuse. I was terrified to leave fearing he would track me down. At the time, running back to the streets was the safest way to get away from him. Eventually, he was able to track me down and found out where I lived. Now here I am with a broken back and a fractured arm. He's a coward. I'll tell you that. Do you know how much harder it is to get around when you're living on the streets when you can't even walk?"

38% of all domestic violence victims become homeless at some point in their lives, and over 90% of homeless women have experienced severe physical or sexual abuse at some point in their lives.[8,10]

> " Domestic violence is what forced me to live on the streets, and harassment and abuse are what forced me to find housing again. "

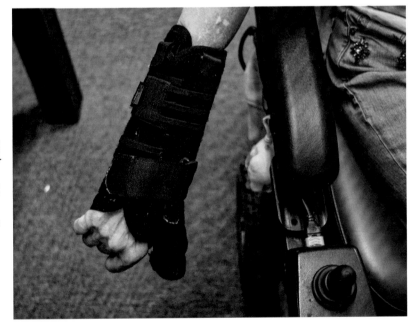

"It's a vicious cycle out here; dog eat dog. People get frustrated. No wonder people have been found in dumpsters. If you were out there experiencing what we experience, I think you would understand our anger and what it is like living in constant fear. I'm still a human being; I put my pants on one leg at a time. I eat, I sleep, I bleed, I cry. I still have feelings just like you, but if you're homeless or low-income, the person-to-person respect strangers have for each other vanishes."

IAN, 28
PORTLAND, OR

While only 7% of the population is LGBT, a staggering 40% of the homeless youth in the United States are LGBT.[7,24]

"I had a home, but I was worried because I was insecure with my sexuality, I had an idea in my head that there was pressure on me to have a wife and kids. I realized I was homosexual when I was younger, but I suppressed a lot of it.

In my Christian family, I was raised with this idea that I was bad, morally wrong, and that lead me to think I had something seriously wrong with me psychologically. What is so wrong me and why didn't I think like the rest of my family? Why did my psychological nature push me to have desires that are supposed to be an abomination? What happened eventually was that I 'solved' my problem and these doubts with a lot of drugs, methamphetamine specifically."

"I've been to jail a few times for drugs and shop-lifting. I had to ask myself why I kept going back to jail. I'm bipolar; that's why. I was in lockdown in Reno solitary for 40 days, and that was terrible. I was there because I had been with cellmates before and it had ended badly. My cellmate was coming off of heroin, and he was trying to start touching and feeling on me. This is literally right after they showed me the pamphlets for prison rape, I kid you not. I wanted to talk to the nurse about it. I could not believe it. When I go in there, I have a lot of emotional baggage. I am happier now living on the streets than I was in solitary confinement."

> "Losing your mother is a horrible thing, but when you are dealing with severe and manic depression, to think she may be alive and well off with her son thinking she is dead is something else."

"I had a parent die when I was a teenager. She had a lot on her plate and was just unable to take care of herself emotionally, and I didn't know how to take that. I think I mimicked that with my self-comfort and addiction process. That was taught. When you lose your mind, the first thing you want to do is jump to drugs and run away from reality. I thought, 'Well I'm crazy either way, what does it matter?' I had to reaffirm with myself with what I know about psychology. So thank God for science. I do have certain things about myself I need to watch out for. For a while, I couldn't recognize my bipolar disorder, especially when I was getting high on meth.

When she (my mother) died, I wasn't doing well psychologically at the time. I had just been diagnosed with my bipolar disorder. I was never given a death certificate, so I had all these questions. I had a therapist who looked a lot like her and started thinking, 'Is that her? Did she fake her own death?' Those are terrifying questions to have. Losing your mother is a horrible thing, but when you are in a horrible psychological state, dealing with severe and manic depression, to think she may be alive and well off with her son thinking she is dead is something else. It's even scarier to realize that that was the type of person she was. She was the sort of person who would try to wipe her slate clean; she would take off for months at a time, and I wouldn't know if I would see her again.

Let me tell you. It's a scary thing to lose your mind.

There are bouts of depression and bouts of mania. The depression wants to just isolate while the mania is severe and very intense. But if I take a step back and am able to see the difference between my mood and what's going on with me psychologically, then I can handle it. Every day there are highs and lows to it. It's a temporary crazy; I lived in an alternate reality for a while there."

RICHARD, 61
PORTLAND, OR

"My daughter died four years ago, and I haven't given a shit about anything since then. Call it depression, call it giving up, call it what you like. She died of a medication mix-up from her sleep apnea. She had two different doctors and didn't tell each doctor which medication she was taking, so she was prescribed two that didn't go together. She just went to sleep one night and never woke up. She just stopped breathing.

You never think that simple little mix-ups like that can have permanent effects. I don't feel anything now. I want to exist until my time here is done. My daughter was 26. She was the light in my life. She was daddy's little girl since the day she was born."

"I'm on the waiting list for government housing and have been over a year. In the meantime, I finally found a few people to keep around for protection. We all need protection out here; everything I own has been stolen from me twice since I've been on the streets. You can't blink, you can't fall asleep. You need a group of people to have to take shifts watching each other's stuff. Life isn't easy out here, and making friends isn't much easier."

Over one-third of the United States' homeless population is over 50, compared to just 26% of the general population. These individuals face additional risks in terms of health and safety and are far more prone to develop psychological and physical ailments living on the street.[63]

"I started working at age eight and over 50 years of being in a kitchen has taken its toll. I had a lot of big jobs: a chef for Walt Disney World, and a chef for the Commission Officers Club for Naval War College. I cooked for Dolly Parton, Ron Howard, and Alice Cooper. It's hard for me to get any other kind of work because they look at me and are like, 'You're a chef. Why do you want to work here?' I can't work in the kitchen anywhere. I'll work pushing a broom, but I just can't work in the kitchen anymore."

"My daughter died four years ago, and I haven't given a shit about anything since then."

TERRI, 49
PORTLAND, OR

In 2017, 47,600 people died from overdosing on opioids, with 15,482 of the deaths attributed to heroin. Of the 886,000 heroin users in the United States, 1.7% die from their addiction.[51]

"I take drugs mostly to deal with the pain from my car accident. My ex-husband tried to kill me. He rigged my car by cutting the brake-line. I rammed into a telephone pole and wrapped my car around it. My face was reconstructed. My knee cap basically fell off. I was in the hospital for almost six months. I can walk okay, but if I had to run for my life, I wouldn't make it. I suffer from a lot of chronic pain now. He's in prison for a long time."

> " I've died several times overdosing on heroin... I quit them altogether almost a month ago. "

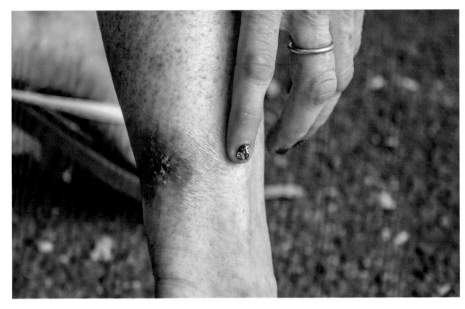

"I fell asleep on heroin with my foot on a camping stove. It burned all the way through my Achilles tendon. It took five months to heal. Those are the dangers of drugs you don't really consider. The pain was unimaginable."

"I've died several times by overdosing on heroin. I got my first abscess on my leg two weeks ago, and it nearly killed me. I was on methadone and heroin. I quit them altogether almost a month ago."

"I came from a dysfunctional family, and there was a lot of crime I saw growing up. I quit school in the ninth grade when I found out I was pregnant; I didn't even know what birth control was. I pushed the saying 'You only live once' to the limit. I say I've lived 12 times. I was 13 the first time I drove a get-away car.

You'd never imagine I have six fully grown children: three boys, three girls, and seven grandchildren. They've all got jobs or are in school. They pay all their bills, own their own houses, they have cars, and they have health insurance. They take care of themselves. They take care of themselves far better than I ever did. They grew up to be responsible adults. I have four fathers to my six children. Three with one man and the other three each have one. They may never believe me, but I am so proud of them."

STEVE, 55
REDDING, CA

"I've been homeless for basically a year. You don't think it can happen to you. I had a good job, and I have two kids. Aging is a very humbling experience. I saw people on the streets before, and I always thought, 'Well they can just get a job, doesn't matter what it is, they can try'- but it's not like that. Maybe they're sick, or maybe they have mental issues. How are you going to get a job with no address or no phone? How do you get to work without a car? You never know what somebody's situation is."

"I'm a mellow drunk. I want to be left alone in my cave. I would just live drunk basically. I eventually realized I need to just do this for myself. It's the hardest decision to make when you are by yourself. I have nobody by my side telling me which direction to take. I have nobody else to blame anymore. I am responsible for changing."

"I'm waiting at the bus stop with all my possessions, and these guys are circling me like monkeys in the Wizard of Oz. They ask me for a smoke, and they ask me how much money I got. I tell myself, 'I'm not falling asleep tonight- no way in hell.' Sure enough, at around 3:00 AM I eventually pass out and wake up with every bit of my life gone.

That was four days ago, but it's just shit. Nothing more. Like George Carlin said, 'When you have shit you always need somewhere to put your shit. Your shit is stuff, and their stuff is shit.' They're all just possessions. It's all shit. You think you need it to live until you keep living without it. All money does is complicate things."

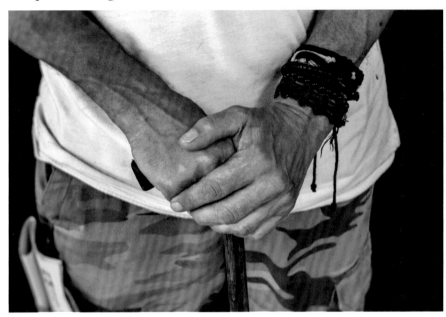

In dealing with isolation and exposure, homelessness is almost always accompanied by elevated levels of stress and anxiety, known triggers of seizures in those suffering from epilepsy.[36,56]

"I look more homeless than you do!"

"Well, what does homelessness look like?"

"I have epilepsy. Alcohol and stress are definitely a part of it. That triggered the last seizure. You just go into this tunnel, and you have no idea how long you have been there, you have no idea what happened, and you leave reality and wake up in the hospital. It's like a slice of death. Your world starts to spin, and you can just tell you're not coming out of it anytime soon. Believe me or not, but I've seen dead friends, and I've knocked on the door- I try to go in, but they just tell me it's not my time yet. Now I get a bracelet for every brush I have with death."

SHEILA, 54
SACRAMENTO, CA

From 2015 to 2017, the estimated homeless population rose approximately 30%, while the number of unsheltered homeless rose 85% throughout that period.[29]

"Practically all my life I used drugs and alcohol. I had a great job working at Walmart until the drugs and alcohol got in the way. I lost my place and ended up homeless. I lost everything. Same old story, but I never thought it would happen to me. That was the worst day of my life: when I had to sleep in the back of the store, on the concrete, on a sleeping bag.

I was on the streets for almost four years. I'm not going to say I got comfortable, but I just got really strung out on drugs and alcohol. As a female, I always felt like someone was watching me because I was by myself. I set up booby traps throughout my camp to keep me safe. I just didn't care about anything anymore. I would panhandle and dumpster dive to provide for myself and feed my addiction. I hated to panhandle. When I did, I had to be drunk already or high. I wouldn't hide anything. I would do it right outside the liquor store."

"I decided I had enough when someone set fire to my camp one day. My dog JJ and I were running, and the guy I was with ran back through the blackberry bushes around the flames just to grab the alcohol in his backpack. That was when I realized I needed a change. The second fire was two weeks later.

The day I went to the AOD (Alcohol and Other Drugs Services), the ranger came up and told me I had to tie up my dog. While I was there, this lady interrupts the class to tell me there was a fire on the river. I could see her face and knew what had happened."

> "It had to take my dog's death to realize I didn't want to be homeless anymore because it could have been me."

"As we drove to the river and I saw where the smoke was, I already knew. It was my camp. It was my JJ. Two years of being on the river and the only day I tie him up there is a fire. The fireman told me they saw a dog running around that looked like mine, so that gave me some hope, but I think he ran back through the fire as I called his name. He was badly burnt. His eyes were burst open, and his nose was peeled up. It was something I wish I never saw. Firefighters brought him to me. He was crying. He was still alive. Right there, I was just thinking, 'Why?' I could've gotten help before, but I just decided I wanted to be homeless because it was comfortable.

It had to take my dog's death to realize I didn't want to be homeless anymore because it could've been me. I wish it would've been me instead of JJ. He was my best friend. I never had a dog that loved me so much. Poor JJ. July 28th made it one year. They cremated him for me, and they didn't charge me one penny for anything. I am really thankful. I have JJ with me, he's on my bed and sleeps with me every night.

At Saint John's, I'm six months and eight days clean and sober. It's a wonderful feeling. It's an amazing feeling. I didn't realize I could do all this, but I'm still recovering. I believe in God and couldn't do it without Him and His guidance. I'm going to graduate from high school and get my diploma. When I move on from here, I'm going to the pound and getting another rescue dog too."

HEATHER
SACRAMENTO, CA

While the average annual cost for permanent housing subsidies and supportive services for a family is $9,000, the average price of placing children of a homeless family into foster care is $47,608. Despite this, 62% of children in homeless families seeking emergency shelter are placed in foster care.[47]

"In 2011, I was in a bicycle accident that landed me in the ICU. My liver was lacerated, and one of my kidneys was damaged. My right lung collapsed, and I was internally bleeding. When I was in the ICU, I was robbed by the people I was staying with at the time. I had all of my things in storage, and they found my key. I returned from the hospital with nothing and no place to live.

I even lost my kids because of the wreck. The Sacramento court system really screwed up. I had full custody of my kids, and their father had never been to a court date in five years. We had been through mediation and he never showed up. I had filed for a domestic violence restraining order that was never picked up on. The courts said that he needed to anger management and parenting classes before he could have visitation of the children. While I was in the hospital, he filed and said I had abandoned our kids and the courts believed it. They granted him temporary custody before going through our case. So, when I got out of the hospital, I got out to absolutely nothing. I didn't even know where my children were.

Because I did not have a place to live, the court extended temporary custody to the father. They've gotten away with it so far because I've had no lawyer and had to represent myself. Unless it's CPS or a criminal case, you are not guaranteed a lawyer. If it's a custody case and one parent can afford a lawyer while the other one can't, whom do you think the kids go to? That's not in the best interest of the child."

> **"Some people face real-life struggles every single day. You could be sitting next to a warrior and not even know it."**

"Eventually, after having my new baby, I felt I had to make a decision to leave my kids where they were because I knew they were safe and well taken care of. Emotionally and mentally, I could not keep going and still be the mom to this new baby. In my head, I didn't know how to do both. I felt this new baby was going to be neglected emotionally. So that's what I did. I put it on hold and became the mom to him that I was to them. That's what he deserved. It was no one's fault. It was just things that happened. I have two kids here with me and still am fighting to get back the other three.

I've learned never to give up. There are people out there with missing arms and legs, and they're parents. They struggle every day, but they still raise their kids. They still go to the store. They still go to school and get degrees. What excuse do we have? Some man with one leg just climbed Mt. Everest. If they can do this, so can we. We have no excuse. Some people face real-life struggles every single day. You could be sitting next to a warrior or tomorrow's hero, and you wouldn't even know it. Dr. Phil was homeless. Obama was raised in a single parent home. Look at where they are today. They had the will, and they knew it. What excuse do I have to give up?"

DAVE & CHARITY
SAN FRANCISCO, CA

"We've been married for two years. We got here by Greyhound. We had our car stolen and totaled in North Carolina, and they made us pay for the tow. That was our mode of transportation and everything we had, but it's a good thing. That was another responsibility, and now we're a little freer and have one less thing to worry about.

We are heading to San Luis Obispo to try to settle down and find jobs and a place to stay. I like to work, I have no problem working, and I have plenty of experience. I could walk into a place and get a job. The problem here is stability, and I couldn't get to work every day. I couldn't give them a number to call."

> "Be sure never to take yourself too seriously. It's okay to laugh. Things will always get better."

Optimism has been linked to a number of both mental and physical benefits, including one's ability to cope with stressors and life problems.[22]

CHARITY: "In some ways, it's nice having no phone and no computer. It's very free. If I want to reach out to someone, I'll send a postcard, and they will be far more excited to get it than getting a text. We saw a couple walking by holding hands, but they were absorbed into their phones. I really doubt they were texting each other, and that's no way to live!

At first, you think its freedom with no mortgage to worry about, no bills to worry about. After a bit though you see how restricting it is, I might not know when my next meal is. I might not know where I'm staying tonight; it's a constant battle."

DAVE: "The cops pulled us over in North Carolina because you're not allowed to hitchhike there. He saw that my flip-flops were shredded to the point where my feet were getting torn apart from walking, so he spent forty bucks of his own money to get me peroxide and bandages and all that. He was one of the nicest people I've met.

Since I've been homeless, I've learned to just drop the ego and drop the self-importance. Be sure never to take yourself too seriously. It's okay to laugh. Things always get better. We are in one of the worst situations, and we're enjoying life more than most people I see passing by.

We just like to make people smile. Some people who will come up and give us a dollar even though it looks like they need it more than we do, so I'll turn them down. We just want to make them laugh, the laugh we get is worth it."

TIM, 20
SAN FRANCISCO, CA

An individual's overall perception of others can indicate a series of personal behaviors and characteristics. A tendency to view others positively, for instance, displays favorable trends such as kindness or empathy.[66]

"Homelessness is a complex issue. You see people struggling, and you see people having a hard time and have to ask yourself, 'How much do I want to help this person get better?' On the other hand, you still have to question their intentions. You have to question if they want to get better. We all struggle with things, and when we see someone struggling, we like to separate ourselves from them. People don't want to see the ugly, but their ignorance is part of the ugly.

People passing me on the street may look at me differently, but it depends on the type of person they are. If a person forms a perception about you without knowing you at all, then that's more of a reflection of them than the person they're judging."

> **"If everyone was always themselves and was willing to learn from others, we could all grow to be better day by day."**

"I try to use my observations of other people to question myself and question whom I want to be. If I see something in someone I don't like, I have to ask myself why. Sometimes it's because I see a part of myself that I don't like, and I have to acknowledge that. When you meet so many people, you're meeting so many parts of yourself and can use that to as an opportunity to self-reflect and empathize with others.

I'm constantly using the world to reflect on myself. Always be you. If you're going to withhold something you were going to say because you're too worried what the other person would think, then you're never going to be able to grow as a person. Not only that but who you're talking to isn't going to be able to learn either. If everyone was always themselves and was willing to learn from others, we could all grow to be better day by day."

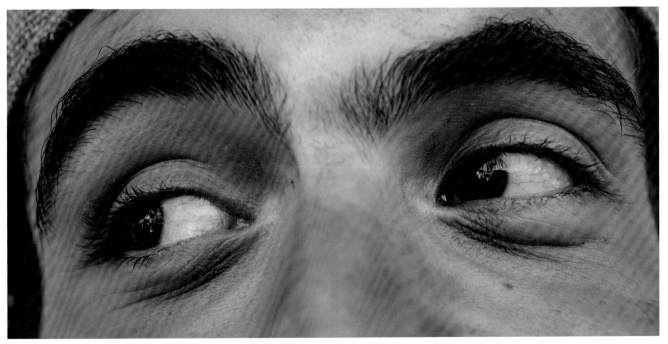

LEE, N.A.
LOS ANGELES, CA

The creation and production of visual art has been proven to improve psychological resilience significantly and even lower an artist's cortisol levels, otherwise known as the stress hormone.[14]

"I came out here in search of answers to questions, but I've realized there are really no questions. You just be. I don't need to have a name, a race, or an age. Those things don't matter. Freedom brought me here. Georgia is still racist. Here I have amazing, beautiful people coming up and talking to me. That would never happen in Georgia.

You can have colors, but if you don't have perspective, then what do you have? People are like, 'I love your hair,' 'I love your outfit.' If that's what you say you love, then what do you really love? When people ask me how I am in the morning, do they really want to know? Or do they just want me to say, 'I'm good.' I'm not up for this surface shit, I want to really get into people's thoughts, I don't care to deal with that. I care to create. I want to create positive thoughts and create more beauty in a world filled with beauty."

"I would rather create things than be talking about issues all the time. I use my art to create and provoke insight. I feel like I'm making a positive contribution to the world. My art plants seeds in people's minds, and if they water it, then they can let it grow. I can't install any positivity in anyone, the responses I receive tell me it's positive or not. If people cry over my work or hand me a green piece of paper as a reward, that tells me it's positive."

"My art plants seeds in people's minds, and if they water it, then they can let it grow."

"We use these languages that we are taught. We use the term 'homelessness' to downgrade people. People can call me homeless, but I'm not. I'm here because it's what is best for me. I've lived in a house, I've lived in an apartment, I've done that. Now I've chosen to come live on the land. Now I have everything.

There's no such thing as homeless. We all live on the Earth. There are just some people who decide to pay more money for square footage. Ten miles down the beach you see people paying millions of dollars to wake up to an ocean view. I sleep in the alley in my tent; it's not luxury, but I know I don't have to pay to wake up close to the shoreline. Nature provides everything we could possibly need. Our Earth is the only thing we need; people just found a way to monetize parts of it."

"Someone came up to me the other day and told me a kindergartner could paint this, and that was really the first time I looked at this painting as something special, that's when I started to love this piece. To be able to recreate anything with the mindset of a child is special to me, it's innocent. Everyone needs to try to hold on to the kid in them because that's where creativity starts."

LONE WOLF, "OLDER THAN DIRT"
LOS ANGELES, CA

In 2009, 47% of homeless veterans served in Vietnam. At this point, the average age of a Vietnam veteran was 63 years old. [32,57]

"I've been out here 37 years. Before that, I was in Vietnam killing people. That's all I did, I feared for my life, and I killed people. And I'm not going to say another word about it. I came out here to clear my head and have been here ever since. I'll likely be out here the rest of my life, what of it there may be. I feel at peace here.

I like to offer people advice in their life from a different perspective and try to diagnose what their problems are if they want me to. It's not like I have some kind of special wisdom, but I think I have an outside perspective from people passing on the sidewalk like yourself."

"Your problems are just beginning. You're going to be running into the ungrateful and the unappreciative on your trip, I can tell you that much. I can tell you that you don't know what you are in for and I can tell you that you are going to come across some things you could not have predicted."

"The people walking by are searching for things to connect with. Everybody's lost. Everyone is looking for entertainment to distract them. I took that feeling and sat on it for years. I was so rattled from Vietnam, and I came here to escape. I couldn't ever put myself into normal society after that. I never thought I would return to living a 'normal' American life. That's not freedom, and I don't need to be out here to feel free, you can feel free anywhere in your mind.

Violence is passed down from generation to generation. Our fathers killed people, and their fathers killed people, and so forth. More often than not, it's for power or land rather than social good. People don't need to be violent. I always say, 'Don't make a wave until you have to.' Be true to yourself and be as good as you can."

> "The people walking by are searching for things to connect with. Everybody's lost."

THOMAS, 29
SAN DIEGO, CA

"I've been on and off the streets for a while now. I choose it; it's a good life. I come from a strict family and to be out here, to be free, it's an adventure. I get beachfront property for free! The world's our oyster. I travel up and down the coast all the time. There are people from my hometown that are doing the exact same thing they were ten years ago. Except they have a job, a little more permanent of a lifestyle, make a little more money, but they haven't moved: they haven't done anything.

I've learned to have gratitude for a lot of things out here. Life's not about what you have or your material things. It's who you are and what you do as a person. Your intentions. That's what really matters. It's not the kind of car you have, how big your house is, what type of job you have that's important in the long run. I feel the more all of us learn that the less likely we'll spend so much money on simple materials and things like Gucci bags and Tom Ford sunglasses. You can leave whenever you want and go back to that square life, sit inside that square box, staring at a square screen. Everywhere there are squares."

> **"**I live by the Nietzsche quote, 'Those who were seen dancing were thought to be insane by those who could not hear the music.'**"**

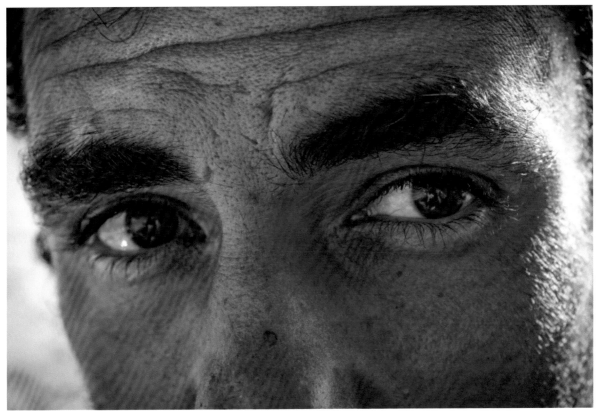

Consumers with materialistic tendencies have been shown to face a greater risk of depression. Those who prioritize wealth and possessions tend to be less satisfied in life and even experience fewer positive emotions in any given day.[20]

"People that look at me on the streets might be upset; others may be curious. They work hard for their stuff, and they like what they have. They make payments on their cars and rent payments. I seem to be having just as much fun if not more fun than they are, but they don't want to give up what they worked hard for to have this freedom, and I understand that. I live by the Nietzsche quote, 'Those who were seen dancing were thought to be insane by those who could not hear the music.'

This adventure has come with its struggles though. Many people out here struggle with addictions with alcohol, heroin, all that. Alcohol had me really messed up for a while. A big eye-opener for was to see so many of my friends out here die from overdosing, cirrhosis of the liver, drunk mistakes, and murdering each other over drugs. There are dangerous temptations to this lifestyle, and luckily I strayed away from that before it was too late."

JOHNY, 44
LAS VEGAS, NV

"Some of us are just here because we make bad choices. I've been on the streets for nine months now. I can get around on my own. I'll find something in a dumpster and fix it up to sell. I've always been handy. I can fix about anything I touch. I'll just find somebody to buy it. I don't need to rob, steal, cheat, or lie to get it. My grandpa always said the best place to find a helping hand was at the end of your own arm. I get all my shit legitimately and honestly. If I do without, it's because I messed up. I was too high and didn't do anything. I've owned businesses. I've been a home builder, a framer; I just need to get certified here to do it."

"I was in a foster home when I was five and six. After that, I was adopted and lived in a poverty-stricken home with a drunk hillbilly stepfather and a strict religious mother. I was in poverty and hungry, so I started selling dope. I made a good living doing it and never got caught, but I ended up here so what does that tell you."

Although the homeless population in Las Vegas has dropped nearly 34% from 2017 to 2018, the city has the tenth most homeless people in the United States despite being 28th in overall population.[2]

"I've brushed with death quite a few times. I stopped my heart three times by the time I was 21 just from overdosing. I've been in seven car wrecks where I've rolled my car. I did a lot of dumb things. I went to prison for eight years for carrying concealed weapons. It felt like forever and a lifetime. I was selling guns and dope, and that's when I quit. I've just made bad choices. I've made mistakes. I knew better; I just didn't care. I take responsibility for the position I am in. I put myself here. Now it's too late to care. I have asthma, bronchitis, the first stage of emphysema, and chronic obstructive pulmonary disease. That's just my life.

I'm at rock bottom. That's how I feel sometimes. Sometimes I just want to blow my brains out and be done with it. Fate tells me there's some reason to hang around. I still get high. I know what I'm doing is wrong. I like the dope. I like the way it makes me feel. That's why I liked it when I was young. I just felt like I didn't fit in anywhere, so I got high and would fit in with everybody. Now you sit back and look at all you've lost and how you let yourself become what you've become. I live a lot in the past. I do that because I'm scared to look towards the future. I've been sick for nine years, I don't have much time left, and I don't have much hope for myself."

> **"I take responsibility for the position I am in. I put myself here."**

SCOTTY, 50
FLAGSTAFF, AZ

Domestic violence is the third most common cause of homelessness in the United States, with 16% of homeless individuals suffering from abuse.[41]

"My siblings have homes, and they know I'm homeless. They help out. I have four brothers and two sisters. There were thirteen of us, but six died in two separate house fires. My dad came into the house with a gas can, stuck it next to the stove, and it caught on fire and killed five. This one was before I was even born. After that fire, we moved from Louisiana over to Flagstaff, which was where I was born.

My mom was with my dad for basically all my life but died of pneumonia in 1997. My dad just died earlier this year from cancer. When my dad moved to Arizona, there were eight kids. Then a second fire happened. My older sister died after she went back into the house to save the Bible. I rolled underneath the stove. That's how I survived the second fire. They didn't know I was in there."

"My parents raised me well. My dad gave me a house, and I burned it down with some crack smokers. I watched it burn down. I left to go to the store and came back, and it was just in flames. That was a horrible feeling. My father gave me that house and I let it burn to the ground, and I'm homeless now because of it. I've seen far too many house fires in my time. I'm sober now, and that's a great feeling to be able to say that, I just wish I did sooner. I've worked in the past at NAU and a few other places around here but had a heart attack last year and was told I couldn't do any heavy lifting."

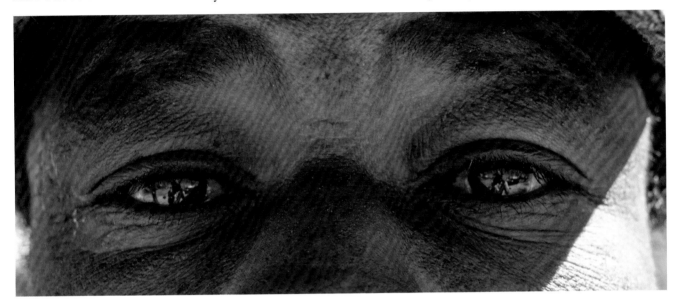

"In the near future, I want to see myself back in school. If I can convince my wife. She thinks I'm always with other women if I'm at school. She is incredibly jealous. I'm a friendly person, and she always thinks the worst of me. But if I can convince her, I want to do computer pro-gramming- that's what I was going for before. I was going to community college and working at Outback, but she thought I was cheating on her cause I would be out work-ing late. Don't ever marry a jealous woman.

"I have four brothers and two sisters. There were thirteen of us, but six died in a house fire."

My wife is probably my biggest struggle in being homeless. I had a good job, I was going to school, but she couldn't handle it. She always thought I was with other women when I would be in class or at work. When you say 'I do' to a woman, you go through with it. The way I was raised, you don't cheat on a woman. I'm a one-woman man. She would still stay with me if I went back, but I don't want to listen to all the crap. She gets physical."

CAMI, 49
ALBUQUERQUE, NM

DISCLAIMER: In my interview with Cami, it was clear she was suffering from a severe mental illness. She struggled to stay on track with her thoughts and often appeared visibly shaken. These are her own words from her interview and should be read with regards to her mental health.

"I've been homeless since 1998; it's been a long haul. I'm homeless because my identity keeps getting stolen. There are people, people who act like me and say they're me. I entered the psychiatric system in Arizona and was in a ward for eight months. I was first diagnosed with schizophrenia, but they went through several diagnoses. I don't know what I have now."

> **"I was first diagnosed with Schizophrenia, but they went through several diagnoses. I don't know what I have now."**

"I had two kids, both from C-section. But when the nurses came back, they didn't bring my children to me. They switched them; they gave me someone else's kids. I didn't want that. I wanted them extinguished, just like my father wanted me extinguished. They didn't treat me like I was theirs. I couldn't hang on to them. I started off taking care of them even though they were someone else's. Every two hours I was breastfeeding her until I got her on a bottle. But she didn't like it. So, I started letting her cry for herself, and I started drinking and not caring for her. I was smoking six packs a day and then started smoking twelve packs a day. I let her fend for herself. I wasn't financially stable or mentally stable anymore. I started being immature about it. Eventually, I went to court and CPS took them away."

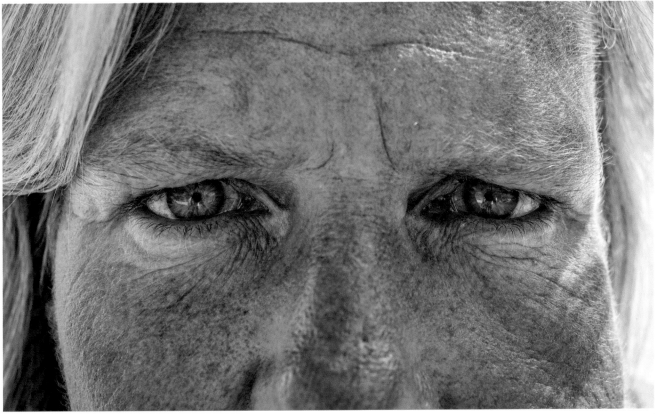

Although schizophrenia only affects a little more than one percent of the United States population, an estimated 10-25 percent of homeless people suffer from the disease, six percent of the entire Schizophrenic population.[49]

"My upbringing was horrible. My mom had cancer when she was carrying me. My dad wasn't allowed to come to my appointments because he wanted me terminated. He didn't want me to be born because they thought something was wrong with me. I wasn't supposed to be born.

My dad was not my natural father. I was always smacked in the right hand so I would be left-handed when I was a child. My dad wanted me to be like him. My dad would fornicate with me in front of my brothers without taking my virginity. He said it was okay that way. My older brother would shoot me up with meth. I was raped over seven times. He would say things like, 'I'm going to do this to you, I'm going to make you bleed."

STEPHANIE, 25
EL PASO, TX

"I became homeless when I lost my father in 2009 to cancer. I was really close with him, and that hurt a lot. I was living with my mom after that but my step-dad over-drank to the point where I just couldn't deal with it.

She (the dog) is for my autism. I have high-functioning autism on the Asperger's side of the spectrum. It affects your socialization skills, but it affects me mostly emotionally. With autism, you handle emotions through repetitive nature: I will bang my head against the wall when I'm really agitated. She will start whining, yelping, and will lick me to get my attention. If I have a bad dream, she'll lay on top of me like a security blanket. It's even harder being homeless when you have autism because it's so difficult to communicate with people. I feel lonely a lot of the time, and when I need help, it's almost impossible for me to get my message across to someone willing to listen."

"The first time I was diagnosed with leukemia, I was ten. It lasted until I was 16. It came back when I was 20 and in and out of shelters. I was carrying a kid at the time as well so at first, they couldn't do any treatment. Luckily it wasn't as strong as it was the first time, I didn't need to do chemo like I did when I was younger. Though the radiation therapy I got makes your skin very fragile, so it bruises easily.

I was carrying my son at the time, and my daughter, Annabelle Marie is the oldest at three. I gave her up for adoption since I couldn't take care of her at the time. I still keep in contact with the family. It was a little hard, but I understood I couldn't take care of her. I was carrying her while I was homeless as well. When I was about a week off from her due date, I went to a place where homeless or impoverished people who can't take care of their kids go to put them up for adoption. I did the same thing with my son, Lauren, who is almost two."

Parents who have a psychiatric disability lose custody of their children as often as 80 percent of the time.[55]

"**With autism, you handle emotions through repetitive nature: I will bang my head against the wall when I'm really upset.**"

"I wish people would be more understanding to be able to help people like us. All they really say to us is to get a job. That doesn't help us. Most job places won't give us work. Even if I could work, I couldn't get a job with my ID being stolen and no contact information. Homeless people are not the only ones who are targeted for things getting taken from them, but they think the homeless are the ones that are going to steal it from them. That's not true. I've had my things stolen from me by people who aren't homeless.

Truthfully, most homeless youths are not out there to try and hurt people. We want to be understood by everyone. We don't want anybody else to be homeless, and we aren't going to cause anybody else to be homeless. It's not a fun life. It's very painful and harsh. It makes most of us sad. I can tell that people are afraid of us. They don't actually show it, but that's what it feels like. You have to learn to keep your hopes high but still wait for the worst and expect to have a lot of doors slammed in your face."

JOHNNA, 55
BATON ROUGE, LA

"I spent six years in prison for stealing aluminum. It's as dumb as it sounds- don't steal kids! I met a lot of people there who weren't lifelong criminals, just people who made a few bad mistakes, and it cost them their lives. Six years felt like a lifetime, and I'm still doing time. I lost everything; I'm bound right here under this bridge.

I've got more than most right now. I've got my little setup, but what else am I supposed to do with it? I didn't plan on living under this bridge; I didn't plan on having to get rid of most of my possessions. I had many things that were really sentimental to me that I had to just let go of. This makes me a target for people around here. Trust me. It doesn't matter how little you have; some people are always going to find a way to steal from you. I know... you're going to go on about the irony of a thief having to be worried about thieves- I see it, and I paid for my mistakes already- well that's what they tell you!"

While circumstances vary, it takes an average of three months to be approved for disability and another two months to receive the first check. In addition, the poverty rate for those living with a work-limiting disability is three times greater than those living without a work limitation.[39]

"I finished serving my sentence and used the money I had left to rent a short-term lease on the cheapest apartment I could find. I took the things I had left out of storage and started looking for a job. Nothing. Not a callback, not a follow-up interview, nothing. There's a joke I was told in prison that the only way a felon can get a job is if they work for free. That was no joke. Sooner than later my money ran out and now I'm paying for my sins under this bridge like a damn troll one day at a time. I've been here for almost a year."

> " **I'm waiting on hearing back about disability, if prostate cancer is what gets me out of here, then I'll consider it a blessing!** "

"Just before I moved out, I went to the doctor for a routine checkup and was diagnosed with prostate cancer. I'm taking it one stride at a time, I do my best to make it to radiation appointments, and it's in its early stages so luckily there is not much left to do. I wait day in, day out, and age day in, day out. I'm waiting on hearing back about disability. If prostate cancer is what gets me out of here, then I'll consider it a blessing!"

JOHN, 53
NEW ORLEANS, LA

"My name is John Fitzgerald Kennedy. I was born two months after JFK was assassinated and was named after him. I used to be a cop. I retired early and managed my brother's bar for four years. I stopped working when I injured my knee, and everything went downhill from there. I was in a bad place and was struggling with alcohol. Eventually, I wore out my welcome, and my friend dropped me off at a psych ward. I stayed there for eight days in recovery and have been homeless for the last month.

I can't even walk, let alone work. I dislocated my knee twice, tore all the ligaments, and have broken my kneecap. Though I'm waiting on disability, I need a new kneecap if I want to be healthy again."

"I sit out here on the corner all day with my back against the wall, but I can't ask people for money. I tried it one day and just started crying; I just can't do it. I have that pride in me that I just can't seem to swallow. I wonder what my niece and nephew would think of Uncle John if they saw him like this. I stopped speaking to my family since I've been on the streets; I can't handle having to talk to them."

"This is a dark place to be where you are surrounded by people but still feel alone."

"A mom pulled up to the light with her kid, and I hear, 'Mommy look!' 'Don't look at him!' she said. Everybody's got issues, and we all have feelings, we don't need to always be looked down upon. We're just homeless. I'm not looking to make friends or anything. I'm just trying to survive."

Homeless individuals are over 430 times more likely to commit suicide than the general population, with a study finding 5.8% of homeless individuals ending their lives via suicide compared to the general population's rate of .013%.[15]

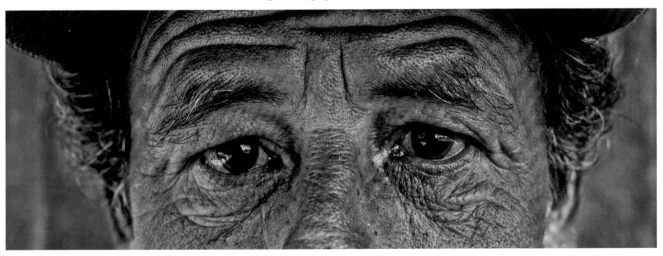

"How much lower can you get than this? When I was in the psych ward, they asked me if I was suicidal. Yeah, I want to blow my fucking head off. If there were a 9mm sitting on the counter, I would've locked and loaded and blown my fucking head off. This is a dark place to be where you are surrounded by people but still feel alone."

21

LEROY, 54
NEW ORLEANS, LA

"I came out here in 2008 looking for some work after Katrina. I've been homeless for about seven years, on and off of alcohol. It's tough living on the streets when you have trouble moving or lifting anything more than five pounds. I get disability because I got ruptured cartilage from a car wreck in my spine. That would pay for an apartment, but I need to get clean before I can do that. I was for seven months until about two months ago when I lost Mary, my wife of five years. I was staying with her at her apartment at the time. I'm a very sad man now that she's gone. I wish I could have saved her. She froze up and just couldn't breathe. I was right there. I was laying on the sofa and woke up, and she was in the freezer putting ice on herself. It almost happened about 10 days before that, but the ambulance got there in time. I called the ambulance when I saw her and had to call back three times. They took 22 minutes to get there. She was dead in 12."

> **"** I'm a very sad man now that she's gone. I wish I could have saved her. She froze up and just couldn't breathe.**"**

"She died of a heart attack. My heart has been racing ever since. I gave her mouth to mouth, but she was gone. I was on the phone with 911 talking to her. She made this loud, horrible groaning sound and just stopped breathing. I've never seen anything like it. I don't have anything from her, no pictures, nothing. The landlord set everything out on the sidewalk and thieves took it all."

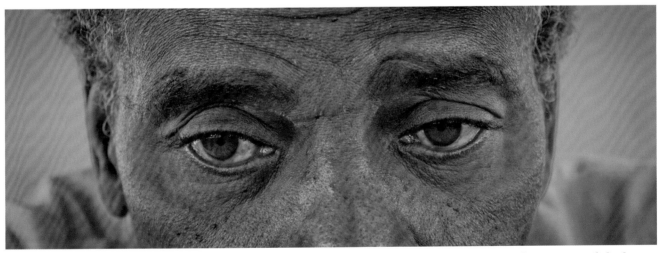

While African Americans make up only 11% of the overall veteran population, they make up 31% of the home-less veteran population.[37]

"I'm a veteran on disability, the usual story with a veteran you see out on the streets. I was in Armor Crew for five years. I was a tanker and always worked in tanks. I've been a gunner, a loader, and a driver. M60 A1's, M48 A3's, A4's- big tanks with the guns on them. I was Assistant Manner too. I started out at Fort Knox. I took my boot camp and AIT at Fort Knox, Kentucky. My first duty station was Fort Carson, Colorado. I stayed out there for about 26 months and then went to South Korea."

22

JOHN, 52
TALLAHASSEE, FL

Adults who were raised in a culture of sexual or physical abuse are 26 times more likely to become homeless than individuals with no history of abuse.[34]

"I worked as a HUD supervisor for over two decades, checking houses for low-income people. One day I was basically told I was either being fired or going to have to quit due to budget cuts. I worked all my life for that and that kind of just put a damper on everything I worked towards.

I've had epilepsy my whole life. It's caused from being beaten in the head throughout my childhood by my father. I had a very rough upbringing. One day I was sitting on my mother's lap when I was seven, and she was shot in the head. The bullet went through her into my skull, and it's still there today. It was so lodged in my skull that doctors couldn't take it out. Somebody drove by and just blew a hole in her head, just a random thing. Four bullets hit my mother in the head, and I could feel the heat of her blood splash over me. Since then, I've had some severe sleeping problems and have fought with flashbacks."

"The epilepsy simmered down when I turned 14, but when I got to 40, it hit me like a brick. I spent three and a half years in a nursing home. That was the worst experience of my life. I lost movement in a hand and my leg. I finally got disability for my condition, so I know I won't be out here forever. I'm on so much medication for my seizures that I have trouble functioning. I still have them from time to time. I'll just wake up, and I've pissed myself or shit myself. Other people will look at that and just assume I'm drunk."

"I have three kids who are full-grown. I haven't seen them since they were children though. When I was splitting up with my wife, I was told by my lawyer that I would not be able to get custody and the best thing to do was just give them space. That tears me apart every day. My brother, who was a preacher, and his wife were looking after them as well for a long time, but he hung himself in his garage. I learned why soon after: he was raping my two daughters. I still keep tabs on them, and it weighs on me heavy that my daughters were raised in the same revolving door system that I was. I want to go see them, but what would I say?"

> "When I was seven, I was sitting on my mother's lap, and she was shot in the head."

"At my age now, people just look at me like I'm an alcoholic or an addict, and I'm neither of those things. I'm just struggling to live here. It's late afternoon, and I haven't eaten since yesterday. I get my new food stamps tomorrow. Not all homeless people are bad people. People look down on homeless people or drug addicts, but how would they handle certain situations? And how would I handle someone's situation who has been out here for a year and was raped their whole life? I used to buy Jack Daniels by the gallon after I lost my kids. I brought myself out of that, and I just told myself that I'm not going to be controlled by alcohol anymore and that was it. The withdrawals were horrifying. I was puking up blood; at times I couldn't even move because of the pain. A lot of people out here went through very similar struggles but just can't talk about it. That's why some of them drink themselves into oblivion."

23

PATRICK, 68
TALLAHASSEE, FL

"I think a lot of the homeless people out here have some sort of disability. From Schizophrenia to Bipolar Disorder, you name it. I'm PTSD myself. I started having my problems as early as '78 when I was first hospitalized at the VA. I have been in and out of the VA about seven times since then. I had previously suffered from anxieties and extreme paranoia for over six years. Medication and therapy have helped me overcome most of it.

Since I've been here, I've been in the hospital three times. Two of the visits were for beatings, and the other was for an anxiety attack. The first time I was beaten, I didn't even know what happened because I was so heavily medicated. I wasn't fully conscious, but I only remember my eye being sewed up. I was given this medication called Seroquel that is supposed to knock me out and prevent night terrors and flashbacks. The issue is when I stay awake under the medication I suffer from psychosis. I'm capable of wandering off evidently and will invade other people's camps. Around here, that's basically asking for a beating. I have had my PTSD prescription stolen from me both times I have been beaten."

"I fought in Vietnam. When you're there, you know you're there cause there's no other place that looks like it. We went from one operation to another. I started manning the Vietnamese Demilitarized Zone where there was no crossing from north to south. And then after a few months, I was attached to another group that was a special force. We were basically a lookout or a hit squad. If someone wasn't supposed to be there, that's where we were sent. They'd pick us up by helicopter, drop us off, and we'd go out and get them."

"In Vietnam, I saw a lot of massacres. I learned to live in fear. I mean, what can you do besides deal with it?"

Over 9% of all homeless adults are veterans. Despite a slight rise from 2016 to 2017, homelessness among veterans has actually dropped 45% since 2009.[30]

"There isn't some specific experience from where my PTSD came from; it was just the whole experience. You live with a lot of uncertainty of who's going to die from one day to the next. We always knew where we were going because that's the area that was being shelled. When companies were overrun, you'd go there the next day to pick up the pieces of soldiers that were left behind or to keep a lookout so other people could pick up the dead soldiers. That was just my way of life there. I saw a lot of massacres. I learned to live in fear. I mean, what can you do besides deal with it? Where are you going to go? I took an 18-hour flight to get there, and home was an ocean away."

24

EVA, 49
TALLAHASSEE, FL

DISCLAIMER: In my interview with Eva, it was clear she was suffering from a discernible mental illness. While she was able to articulate her emotional state, Eva's story was inconsistent, and she appeared to be uncertain of her own past. Most notably, she seemed to be disconnected from her own surroundings to an alarming extent. Because of her indifference for her personal safety, I've chosen to include Eva's thoughts on her own mentality, along with a short narrative, to illustrate the first-hand dangers of being mentally and emotionally compromised in a hazardous environment.

"I'm from Armenia originally, but I was smuggled here illegally by people who were not my real parents. The last time I saw my son and daughter was back at a shelter in 2006. I don't know where my family is now, and that left me depressed for a long time. I met a guy in Seattle, and I thought we fell in love. He took me all the way here and just left me here. I've been in Tallahassee ever since."

> **"I think when people see me, they think I've had a lot of bad things happen to me in my life, and that's not really surprising to hear."**

The lifetime risk for violent victimization for homeless women with a mental illness is 97%, making sexual violence a normative experience for this population.[31]

"Dealing with depression when you are out here is very difficult. I was told not to hide it and express my thoughts and feelings, so I don't get too antisocial and keep it a secret. There aren't a lot of people out here who want to hear it, and that just makes it worse. I'll talk to myself if I have to. Sometimes I'll feel so disturbed, I just feel like I have to run. My depression has gotten a little better since I left the shelter, I couldn't handle so many sad people in one tiny place. Since then, I'm trying to pay attention to all my thoughts that I feel like will be helpful for me and rid myself of all the tragic and hurtful things. I've been trying to give power to hope and not let my depression reign over my intellect."

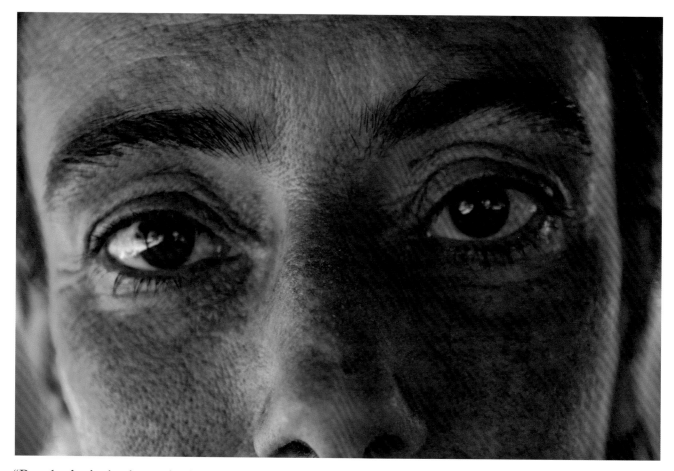

"People don't think much about me being homeless. A lot of people around here are homeless, so we have our own community here. I think when people see me, they think I've had a lot of bad things happen to me in my life, and that's not really surprising to hear. I've been raped twice since I've been out here. A lot of us have had something bad happen to us. People aren't going to like you with your camera questioning people out here. They don't like strangers, and if you are questioning people, they might get weary. You'll need to-"

Eva's statements were interrupted by a scuffle that broke out at the table next to us, about five feet away. After an apparent dispute over acquiring money for crack cocaine, one man pulled out a knife and lunged at the other's neck. Two other men, who had been a part of their conversation, intervened and struggled to gain control of the weapon as the blade was just inches away from the man's neck.

As I sat back in shock fearing for my own safety, Eva remained calm as she continued to eat her sandwich. She spoke quietly, "Guys, you're supposed to be nice to each other." As expected, her words of peace did little to quell the situation. As the struggle continued, she turned her back to the fight and continued with her thought as if she hadn't just witnessed such a violent act. The fight was dispersed when a cop car pulled into the park.

Half an hour later, as our conversation continued, the original aggressor approached our table and began questioning me. With the assumption that I was 'taking advantage of homeless people,' he began making ambiguous threats, asking me where my van was, and telling me interviewing the homeless is 'How motherfuckers get their brain bashed in.'

It is important to note here that I had previously met a news crew at this park for an interview per their request to capture genuine footage. This was a misstep on my part for flippantly dismissing complications that can arise for choosing such a time and place. While the man's suspicions and defensive measures were understandable, his belligerent threats were unwarranted. Again, Eva completely ignores this menace and even attempts to speak over him to continue her story.

I have no authority to speak on Eva's mental state and can only detail anecdotal evidence and expand on my personal opinion. Whether it's a misplaced trust, desensitization, or something beyond my rudimentary psychological understanding, Eva's nonchalant attitude towards safety showed me a new side of the risks of coping with mental instability while homeless, where even instinctual behaviors seem to have taken a back seat. Your reaction may differ, but I see this story as a totem to the additional dangers faced by homeless people suffering from a mental illness.

25

TROY, 55
ATLANTA, GA

"I've never been homeless before. My last living situation didn't work out like I had hoped, and I just found myself on the streets, simple as that. I needed to take a step back and humble myself but keep my confidence. I'm starting to persevere through all these trials and tribulations instead of just falling back and feeling sorry for myself. I'm doing something about it. I can't do it overnight; it's taking time. I have no complaints, though. It humbles me. Struggles are life's opportunity for an individual to build character."

> **"Struggles are life's opportunity for an individual to build character."**

"Not everyone in a bad situation is a bad person. Being homeless is rock bottom. Everyone who finds themselves in their own bottom one way or another. I lost my house, my truck, and my land. That's my bottom."

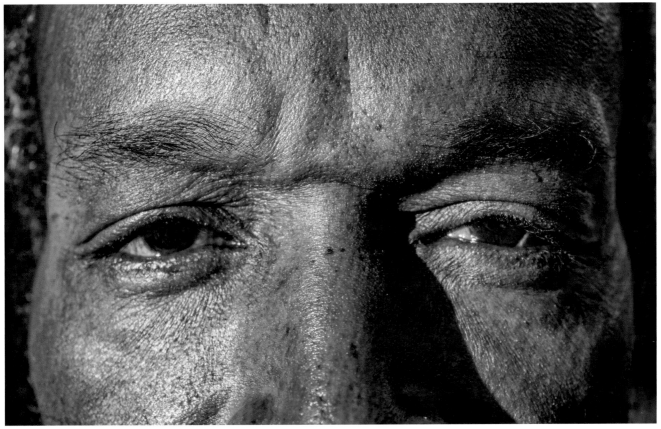

The vast majority of Army soldiers that served in the Iraq War experienced a high level of PTSD-related stressors such as seeing dead bodies (95%), being shot at (93%), being ambushed (89%), and knowing someone who was severely or mortally wounded (87%).[35]

"I was in the Army as a combat engineer, 12th Bravo. I served in Iraq, Saudi Arabia, and Kuwait. We would clear minefields, lay mines, pave the way for tanks, all that. Our life expectancy is three to four seconds in the area. When we clear mines we couldn't use metal detectors, we had to use our hands. I was in Iraq for over two years. I got three bronze stars, and I survived. I still have nightmares but when you survive all that you don't have too much to complain about.

I do have PTSD. I can't be around fireworks. I can't be around a crowd of people. If I go to a restaurant or anything, I got to have my back facing everybody. I don't like people being behind me. I don't like people scaring me or tapping me on the shoulder. It usually leads to violence. I have an anxiety disorder, I get migraines, and I can get paranoid in a split second. I always know my surroundings. I'm still on edge. It is what you make of it. I'm living with it and making progress every day."

26

WENDELL, 55
ATLANTA, GA

"I was in a loving household with a wife and children, but I had a history of drugs and alcohol that kept coming up. Each time I went out, I got worse and worse. I would find myself on the street begging for money. I always told myself I would never do that, but it came to that. Living on the street is hard. I'm not really a street person. At my age, you don't get too many chances doing this. The older I get, the harder it gets. I need to learn from my mistakes instead of punishing myself. They call it insanity. It's insanity to do the same thing over again, knowing that this might happen, expecting different results."

> "I tried twice letting the exhaust run in the car, but it didn't work. I never told my wife and family."

"I have a history of bipolar depression. I can't use that as an excuse; I can't blame anything. I know people who manage bipolar disorder without using drugs. Bipolar depression is like being down in the pits, and there's no way to get out. I just feel bad about myself. I have attempted suicide. I was in the lows all the time; I wanted to get myself out of there. There's a way out, but I stay stuck mentally. Suicide was my escape. Then my flight was drugs, and it didn't make it any better. I tried twice letting the exhaust run in the car, but it didn't work. I never told my wife and family. Today is better, but I need to be a lot more patient with myself. There aren't too many opportunities out here to stay clean and sober. I need to keep focused and thankful. I can't get off course.

Addiction is a monster. When I start to take drugs, I just wanted more, more, more. I wanted to get back that high again. I wanted to stay like that. Regardless of where I'm at, I wanted to stay high all the time. It eliminates depression and the stuff that went on in my childhood. You get more and more of a craving for it. It's nonstop. I spent everything that I had. I stole from my household. I spiraled out of control, and it led me to eventually losing my home and my car."

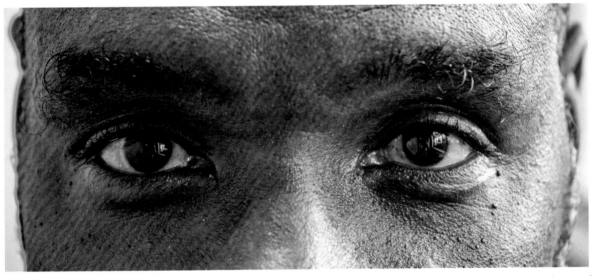

About two-thirds of individuals receiving treatment for substance abuse experienced some form of physical or sexual abuse as children.[65]

"I had an abusive childhood. I grew up without a father and guys around the neighborhood knew that and took advantage of it. I was beaten up. I was molested. That was just what 'growing up' was for me. I never really reflected on it, but it caused a lot of trauma and led me down the path I'm on today."

"I've been clean six months now. I'm taking it one day at a time. I'm back in my own family again, and I'm speaking with my kids. That gives me a lot of encouragement. I still think about drugs. I need to get a stronger network of people to talk to. I tell myself I'm okay, but I'm really not okay sometimes. Interactions with people who have faced and overcome the same struggles you're dealing with saves lives. I'm a veteran, and what they do here is try and transition you out for work and stabilize your addiction. Right now, I'm at the stage of getting another job and getting my own household."

27

DANIEL, 32
ATLANTA, GA

"It started with an alcohol addiction. From there I started snorting cocaine. Then I turned to hard rock cocaine. That's where I had my big fallout. All my morals and everything just flew out the window. My life began to spiral out of control. I was hanging around the wrong people, convincing myself I'm a functioning alcoholic and a functioning drug user. Nobody wanted to be around me. My family said if you don't want to help yourself, how are we going to help you? I was in denial. I always told myself I don't have a habit.

It's a lonely feeling. You ain't got nothing to show for it. You wake up knowing you had $200 or $300 in your pocket and now you ain't got shit. You don't even know where to start. You don't even remember where you laid down. You just remember you were high last night. You work all week, and by the weekend, you're broke. You got people who take advantage of you because they know you get out of your mind. You find yourself living in abandoned cars and vacant properties."

"I started seeing I wasn't accomplishing anything. The drugs were taking over my life from every angle as I always found a way to blame someone else. You just start noticing your years, and the age starts going higher and higher. Everybody has a gift, and everybody has a purpose. I'm at that stage in my life where I want to know my purpose and why I should be here. I've never been peer pressured. I had a great childhood with two loving parents. You start wondering where the bitter, bad apple on your tree came from. But in the end, only I am responsible for my actions. Everything I tried because I wanted to. I lost everything for what? That one time. That one hit. That one high."

> **"As long as I can stay sober for today, we'll worry about tomorrow when it comes."**

While the human brain is chemically predispositioned to succumb to a drug addiction, some brains are more addiction-prone than others due to their genetically dependent dopamine circuit.[28]

"I came to the crisis center for help, and now I'm 30 days clean. As long as I can stay sober for today, we'll worry about tomorrow when it comes. This guy that's been here for over a year gave me his one-year badge to give me a goal. If he can do it, I can do it. He's been clean for nine years. This badge is me surrendering, letting it go. I have daughters who are looking up to me and a sister who is keeping me motivated. It's a long and difficult process, but life moves on. I want to enjoy the rest of my life. I've got a lot of time left."

28

MARK, 45
CHARLOTTE, NC

Homelessness in Charlotte has increased 13% in the last year, with nearly 40% of homeless people claiming a lack of affordable housing to be the primary culprit.[46]

"I have a pretty severe case of polymorphic light eruption, which basically means my skin is very sensitive to sunlight and I'll get nasty rashes all over my face and neck. This is not the best condition to have when you are homeless in Charlotte. Even when I try to stay in the shade, I'll end up breaking out in these awful rashes. They heal right up, but not so quickly when you don't exactly have a place to seek cover. The way I see it, as long as I'm outside, I'll be stuck with these itchy, godawful rashes!

I'm living without a house because I lost my job. It's that simple, other people might have other struggles, but I just can't find work. The model was to be an apprentice for an employer, learn the trade, then after four or five years, you can go practice the profession. Trade school of any kind isn't even considered an option for kids nowadays in school. Not everyone needs to be an engineer or an architect. Not everyone is cut out for school, and that's okay."

"I'm a lot more worried about the future of our society than I am about being homeless. My main complaint about being homeless is the loneliness aspect of it. People think I'm just this street rat and ignore me as if this is my purpose in life. Homeless isn't who I am; this is just part of the ride that I'm along for. I'm okay with that. Life could always be better for everyone. If I were to get stuck in my own pity party every day, eventually people would start ignoring the invitations if you know what I mean. Misery loves company, but that doesn't mean it goes both ways. I could sleep outside for the rest of my life without a worry, but no person should be subjected to go weeks without having another human interaction."

> **" Our society relies on people, not money. I think people forget that. "**

"We need to wake up and respect this earth and maintain clean water. We are one of the most fortunate countries on earth to have access to clean water and leave it to us to destroy that with pollutants. What happened in Flint, Michigan is not an anomaly, and last I checked it still hadn't been fixed! We have such an easy time taking things for granted that we ruin our necessities out of greed. Our society relies on people, not money. I think people forget that."

29

BETH, 54
RICHMOND, VA

A Harvard study found medical bills to be the cause of 62% of all bankruptcies throughout the United States. Out of 51 countries, the United States is the only highly developed nation not to provide universal healthcare.[5,42]

"I've been homeless for the last six months after I got evicted after the medical bills piled up too high. After my mother died, I found myself depressed. She had heart disease and died from an infection in the hospital. I was devastated. I wasn't really eating, drinking, or moving at all. I let myself get sick and ended up in the hospital. My muscles had withered away. I couldn't even walk because I had been so immobile. I went to therapy for a month to gain back my strength. I didn't qualify for assistance, so the therapy and hospital stay ended up costing me a lot of money I didn't have. Between paying for my mother's medical bills and my own, I just couldn't make rent and ended up on the streets."

> "Nobody should be left without a home because they can't afford their medical bills."

"I never gave homelessness much thought, and certainly never thought it would happen to me. I thought people were homeless from drugs, drinking, or abuse- but I was wrong. I've met a lot of people who have never been homeless in their life and just couldn't afford housing after dealing with the unexpected.

But I've also encountered a lot of situations where homeless steal from the homeless. My purse was stolen one night. It had all my papers: my ID, my birth certificate, my social security card. I felt hopeless at first but eventually found it in a nearby trash can. I pulled out the whole bag- something I would never have found myself doing a year ago- and at least found some of my paperwork. A lot of it had been damaged by the rain, but at this point, most of my things have been damaged by the rain. Not everyone is like that. You just need to get yourself around the right crowd so you aren't taken advantage of."

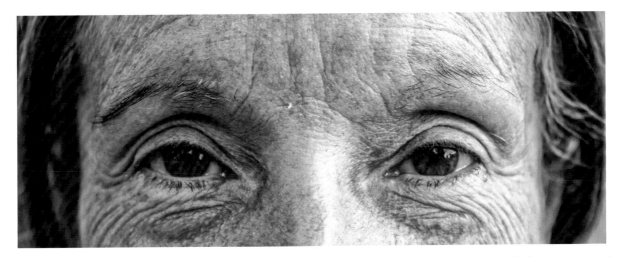

"I know I will get out of this eventually; there are just a lot of hoops to jump through for me to get back into stable housing. The real issue is affordable and stable housing. If housing was more affordable, a lot of us wouldn't be here right now. It's near impossible to have a steady job without having a stable home and just to rent an apartment you need to be able to have enough income to put down a security deposit and first and last month's rent. My parents went through the same thing I did. My father got sick with dementia, and once the medical bills exhausted their savings, my mother had to sell the home. Nobody should be left without a home because they can't afford their medical bills. The best way I can look at it is I'm the last one with the family name, so I know this won't happen to anyone else in my family."

30

ALIAS & DESI, 28
RICHMOND, VA

From 2002 to 2015, the United States saw a 620% increase in heroin overdoses, with heroin being the cause of nearly 14,000 deaths in 2015.[52]

ALIAS: "I wouldn't call myself homeless; home is my backpack. I've got my whole house on my back and don't need to worry about much else. If it doesn't fit in a backpack, you don't need it. We like to train hop to get around. Sometimes you know where it goes, sometimes you don't, but that's part of the adventure. I met some friends who showed me the road and have been traveling since then. You get to see a lot of the most beautiful parts of the country. I get to meet new people everywhere I go."

DESI: "Her original owner checked out on us. He was a drug abuser and overdosed on heroin, so we took her in. Heroin is rough. I've lost a few friends to heroin, including my best friend. It's an epidemic throughout the country, and I've felt like it's been ignored. Some people will look down on us because we have dogs; they assume the dogs aren't healthy or being treated well. I can promise you these dogs are happy and eat a lot healthier than we do."

> **"I wouldn't call myself homeless; home is my backpack. If it doesn't fit on my back, then I don't need it."**

ALIAS: "I had a job, but I completely hated it. You're slaving your life away just to make money just to spend it just to make more money just to spend it. It's a repetitive state of mind to do the same thing every single day. I can't see how that brings you happiness. Wake up, go to work, get off of work, go to sleep, repeat. That's not me. This lifestyle isn't for everybody, but neither is that one, to each their own. I get looked at like I'm the scum of the Earth because of how I live my life. I don't judge a book by its cover until I read it.

Why take life so seriously all the time? You're going to lead your life right into a stressful death. Sometimes I think the signs people want to see would say things like 'Homeless drunk' or 'Need money for drugs' because I think that would at least confirm their suspicions and give them something to be happy about."

DESI: "Some people look at me like 'You're homeless and smiling? What is wrong with you?' That's not to say there aren't any good people though. We get offered help from people all the time. To their credit, we have been around a lot of homeless people, and they vary quite a bit. Some are good, some aren't, just like everyone else in society. I'll give everybody a chance and time of day. I set low expectations for people, but I'll always give people a chance to change that."

31

ARITHOMER, 31
WASHINGTON, D.C.

"I used to work and walk, but ten years ago I caught a disease called avascular necrosis. The disease is relatively rare, but there is no cure. It's most common among athletes because they take steroids. I used to take a type of steroid for my asthma, so that's where the doctor's thought it came from. It stops the blood circulation around your hips so I can walk for about a minute before I have to sit down. When I was first diagnosed, it became so painful where I couldn't even go to work or walk anymore. I went from walking with crutches to a cane, to a wheelchair. There is not a worse feeling than gradually having your own body taken away from you with nothing you can do about it.

After my diagnosis, I couldn't really find jobs that would help me. I ended up homeless in the shelters. There's just really no place for a person in a wheelchair to work. Even though I get some help from the federal government, that is nothing compared to the money you could make from paycheck to paycheck, especially with how expensive DC is. I can't really work any of the jobs offered by the shelters."

"My life has been an uphill battle. I was put in the foster care system when I was a toddler. It is not an easy life when you are that young living with different people all the time. I was always made to be afraid to speak up and believed my voice meant nothing. It felt like torture. I was abused and beaten with coffee mugs, wooden sticks; you name it. I was almost adopted once, but I refused because they wanted to send me to an all-boys boarding school. Sometimes I think that may have been what was best for me. I was kicked out of the foster home at 18 and have struggled with homelessness of and on since then."

Orphans turning 18 and transitioning out of foster care are at far higher risk of becoming homeless than young adults growing up in a stable household. In fact, an estimated 45% of adults leaving foster homes find themselves homeless within 18 months.[25]

"I never thought I would end up homeless. Even when I was sleeping in the streets, I was still in denial. Eventually, I went to a shelter, and that's when the reality set in. Sometimes I feel judged as a homeless person, but I can't let it get to me. Everyone has a gift; I sing gospel for example. A lot of people just go through bad circumstances in life and never get to use it. You never know where people came from and you can never be judgemental when you're asking for help. In spite of it all, I tell myself there's going to be a better day."

> **In spite of it all, I tell myself there is going to be a better day.**

32

SOLOMON, 52
WASHINGTON, D.C.

The homeless rate in our nation's capital is six times greater than the national average. Although African Americans make up only 47% of Washington D.C's population, they make up an astonishing 88% of the homeless population.[3]

"I've got 30 years of being homeless under my belt. When I first came out of high school, my folks and I were never very close. Even from a young age, most of my family had passed away, so all I've had is the man upstairs. I had to raise myself, and that led to a life of going back and forth being incarcerated. My criminal record is the main reason I am homeless."

" Every day out here is a struggle to keep your head above water; don't judge me because of where I sleep. "

"Every day out here is a struggle to keep your head above water; don't judge me because of where I sleep. I go to bed every night and get up around four in the morning every day, go and take a shower, and head to the labor pool to try and get a day's work in. I had a stroke this summer, and that threw me way back. I lost sight in one eye. I don't know when my disability will come in, but I'm trying to take it one day at a time. I pray at night and try to be around positive people. Being out here, you've got to be positive. Since the stroke, I'm slowly losing it a little bit. It's getting hard to even walk without good depth perception. I want to work, but it's disheartening when I struggle through an application because of my eye. I'm a little more paranoid with one eye now, especially at night time. I sleep on the same side as my good eye. So far I've never had any trouble."

"Most of the people that work around here work for the government. They see me make my little bed up when I'm getting ready to lay down. A lot of people talk to themselves about it, some laugh, none approach. Not a single person (aside from you) has approached me and asked why I'm out here. They look down on the homeless. I would think you would get more help being this close to the Capitol, but you don't. I'd like to see them try this for a little while and then try to pick themselves back up from rock bottom. Anybody can be homeless any given day. You could lose your job tomorrow, and you'd end up sharing the same bench beside me."

33

SCOTT, 36
PHILADELPHIA, PA

Philadelphia is not immune to the opioid epidemic. In 2017, there were 1,200 fatal overdoses, and as many as 70,000 Philadelphia residents are addicted to opioids.[59]

"I've had an addiction problem for almost 20 years. It started with alcohol, advanced to prescription pills, and met its peak when I moved out here and was introduced to heroin. I just don't know how to live without it. The only time I'm ever sober is when I go to jail. That's the only time: when I'm forced to. When I'm in jail, the only thing that keeps me going is thinking about getting high when I get out. If not, I'll get depressed."

> **"It didn't matter how hard they tried; I was always going to fail them because I never bothered to try myself."**

"I was in a dependent relationship for about two years before I found myself out here. I met this amazing woman who was supportive and encouraged me to be better. She had her own vices but gave me more chances than I could ever ask for. She was a lawyer and supplied me with housing, clothes, and money. She was trying to rescue me. I would search for jobs, but I never actually applied myself, to be honest. Over time, my drug habits and selfishness wore down her love for me and her patience, and she got sick of it. She kicked me out long after she should have. I'm mad at myself for ruining that relationship; it's hard for me to get over what I did."

"It's painful to take a step back because you see the repercussions of your actions and the toll drugs take on you as a human being. Drugs are the sole reason I am here, and the sole reason I have a record. It's all self-inflicted; I hold only myself responsible.

At this point I don't have anyone in my past in my life, everybody I know is out here. I miss my family. I miss talking to my mom. I know my parents love me, but they don't want to deal with my habits at this point. I was once a year away from getting my bachelors in technology education. Now I'm stuck in a hole that's hard to climb out of. I've pushed away the people who cared about me enough to help. It didn't matter how hard they tried; I was always going to fail them because I never bothered to try myself."

34

BRYAN, 51
NEW YORK, NY

Although African Americans make up just 13% of the U.S. population, they account for 40% of the homeless population.[38]

"I lived in an apartment for 13 years and kept getting sick and didn't know why. Eventually, I pulled back the flooring in my apartment and found that it was covered in black mold. My apartment building didn't have a ventilation system. After months of protests, my landlord refused to clean up the mold or fix the ventilation system, so I began withholding my rent. That got me evicted. That was two years ago, and I've been homeless since then. I now have restrictive pulmonary lung disease from that apartment.

I have a teaching degree from Columbia University and have taught every grade from kindergarten through graduate school. Now when I go into social services or apply for housing, they treat me like the village idiot. You aren't solely responsible for how other people feel about you. I'm not responsible for how others see me; I know who I am. I don't drink, I don't smoke, I don't steal, I don't hustle. I'm not worried about how people judge me."

"People don't realize that homelessness is just what happens when you fall through the cracks. If you ask me, homelessness isn't the issue. Homelessness is what happens when you have a failing healthcare system or mental health services. Homelessness happens when you have an unresponsive VA, or when wages can't keep up with housing costs. Homelessness is just the bottom line to a slew of issues that still need to be addressed.

> "Homelessness is just the bottom line to a slew of issues that still need to be addressed."

It would be interesting to see people try to be homeless for a year. To throw someone in a city where they don't have any contacts and don't have anyone to rely on and force them to make themselves something from the ground up, then check up on them in a year and see what they learned. You learn human nature out here, you learn how to negotiate, and you learn to sharpen your instincts. You learn to evaluate someone in five seconds because now your life might be on the line."

"People argue racism doesn't exist in this country. Racism very much exists; this country isn't cured and probably won't be. The ignorance is taught, and you can't just expect it to go away when blacks get freedom. People wear a Confederate flag shirt, pretending the Civil War had nothing to do with slavery, and insist they aren't racist. I don't think everyone who wears that flag is racist, but do we need a new history lesson? If times passes and people forget, then we are just going to be stepping backward, and that's unacceptable."

35

ANONYMOUS, 54
NORWALK, CT

Alcoholism doubles an individual's risk of developing a major depressive disorder. In fact, 30% of deaths by suicide in the United States were found to have alcohol levels above the legal limit at the time of death.[60]

"I was suffering from bipolar depression. I suffered from irrational highs and intense lows that would happen in a heartbeat. I never knew how depressed I was but the more depressed I got, I drank and the more I drank, the more depressed I got. It was a very vicious circle. I started to hide my drinking. I had alcohol in my workshop, in my van, and in my garage. I didn't think anybody knew. Nobody knew! Right? No. Everybody knew. Things started spiraling downward. I got to the point where I couldn't pay my bills. One day our landlord comes and tells me I need to get out now. That following Monday I rented a moving van and moved out.

In the next 35 days, I would go to a truck stop with the van, get a case of beer, and that was my life. I only had the clothes that were on my back. I started contemplating suicide. Three weeks into this, my older son reported that I had been missing to the police.

I sat in a grocery store parking lot for a week. I would use the grocery store to wash up and just pee in jugs in the van. It was disgraceful. During the last week I was missing, someone in the grocery store recognized me. Unbeknownst to me, they had posters of me everywhere, and my face was all over the news. My son told me they had over 200 people going out looking for me. There were 200 people who cared about me enough to hang up posters and go door to door.

I exit the store, and there are four cops ready to question me. The EMT's came as well, insisting on checking my blood pressure and everything, telling me I was okay to go after that because I had done nothing wrong.

I had a noose tied in the van, which was my plan; those last beers were going to be the end of it. I had figured out how I needed to be positioned for the noose to work because I couldn't stand up all the way in the van.

Right then, I knew that I didn't want to die, but I didn't want to keep living the way I was. There were a lot of angels working that day. That women recognized me in the dark rain and somehow saw me through the scruff and dirt and stink. I surrendered. At that moment, I chose not to walk towards the van where death was waiting for me. When I'm at the hospital, a cop comes in, and I watch his lips say the word 'noose' to the nurse. Once that word broke through the chain of command, it became a much more complicated situation.

> "I had a noose tied in the van, which was my plan; those last beers were going to be the end of it."

That night my life was saved. I was in the psych ward for four weeks. Once I got out, I ended up here sleeping on mats in overflow. It was a shock for me to come here. I didn't know anyone here or this sort of lifestyle. The good people get lost in the swarm of the people you shouldn't trust and realizing that only comes with time. But I'm grateful to be here. I consider this place my second miracle. I feel safe here, and safety is something you take for granted when you have a home."

"For years I was scared, I was afraid of everything and anything. I was in constant fear. I think that was part of the depression, but those fears led me to be who I never wanted to. This place is now part of who I am. It's part of my recovery. This was the best result I could ever ask for. This place keeps me regimented. I get up at a certain time, I get back at a certain time, and I eat at a certain time. I needed that discipline for my recovery.

I'm probably one in a million whose story ended up like mine: good. Homelessness can happen to you in a single moment. 'I never thought it could happen to me.' Use that as your damn slogan for the project."

36

CARMEN
BOSTON, MA

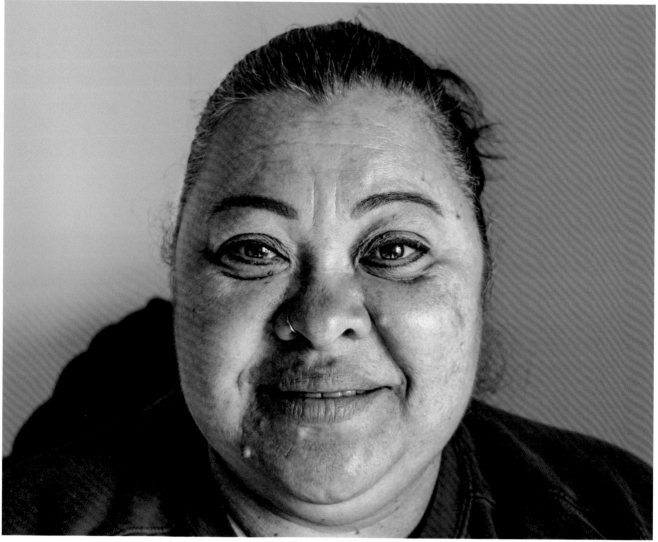

Although only 16% of the U.S. population is disabled, an estimated 40% of the homeless population live with disabilities in the United States.[21]

"I've lived in the shelter system for four years, and it has been very rough. I lived in North Carolina before with my husband, but my condition forced me to come to Boston. Since my surgery, I can walk a little bit, but it is challenging and not having your own place makes it so much harder. I have chronic neuropathy from breaking my spine. I just fell and broke my spine in six places. I stayed in the hospital for a long time and had many surgeries. I have burning pain all over my body and have to sleep with a machine now."

"I never thought I would find myself homeless. Being homeless and handicapped is very sad. People look at me like I have done something wrong. I was a police officer for twelve years and a school bus driver for 25 years. For a long time, I would patrol the streets at night and take off my uniform in the morning and drive the bus. I was a very hard worker and did everything I could to help my family. I'm not the only person who once worked as a professional staying at this shelter, plenty of people work one or two jobs during the day and come here at night to sleep. There are a lot of hardworking Americans and immigrants here."

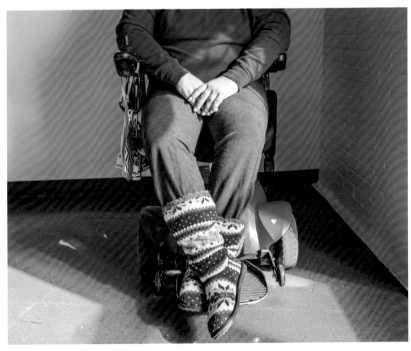

> **"Being homeless and handicapped is very sad; people look at me like I've done something wrong."**

"My son was staying in New Jersey and going to the university there. He left for Puerto Rico and stayed there for a month. I talked to him the day before he was supposed to go home, and that is the last time we spoke. He was shot and killed later that day. He was 22. He would be 25 today. I have two other kids, my daughter has a husband and is doing very well, and my youngest son is studying forensics in college. I may have lost my son, but I've got a lot of daughters here. Everybody calls me 'Mommy Carmen'. I lost one, but I've gained sixty more. I love everybody here."

37

MURIAL, 35
BOSTON, MA

In just one day in 2016, over 31,500 adults and children fleeing domestic violence found refuge in an emergency shelter in the United States. Over 12,000 requests were left unfulfilled due to a lack of resources.[23]

"I have been homeless for a year after I lost my apartment. I had moved in with my mom who was diagnosed with breast cancer to be her caretaker for the nine months before she passed. Once she passed, I only had two months to move out. At the time, I was going through a divorce and fighting an addiction as well, so I decided I couldn't have my kids for the time being because it just was not safe for them."

"I'm the only girl with six other boys. My family migrated from Haiti, a culture where we didn't talk about the things we went through and were always taught not to talk to people about your problems. Depression, PTSD, and alcoholism aren't acknowledged as real sicknesses. They thought I was selfish for talking about my issues, but I just wanted to talk to someone about what was wrong."

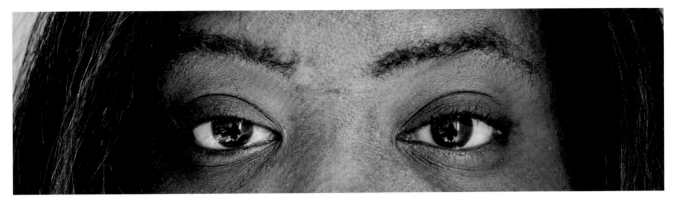

"When I first came to the shelter, I was in a very dark place. I was in a controlling and physically abusive relationship. I wasn't allowed to speak or have any friends. Alcohol was my safe place, and I succumbed to it to escape my reality. My husband would tell me I'm no good and that I can't change or succeed and, for a long time, I believed everything he said to me. I believed my husband when he would tell me I was worthless. I felt like nothing. When I came here, my counselor asked me what I wanted for myself. I told him that I wanted to be happy again. I wanted to be able to see my kids and look in the mirror and see a better person. So, I decided one day to try and change that. My husband didn't like it. I think he saw my personal changes and development as a threat to his control over me. He would hide my shoes so I couldn't go to work, and he would become more physical towards me when I would try to stand up for myself.

Nevertheless, I kept growing. I started opening up bit by bit like a flower. I first came here to get housing so my children could come back to me, but I didn't want to go back to living like I was before and find myself in the same situation again. I started gaining discipline, and eventually, alcohol began to seem less important. I still face struggles, but now when I do, I wear a smile. Five months later and I'm still growing every day. The people here at St. Francis are the saviors who have helped me get through this. I'm now more active with my kids, and my family is noticing changes in me."

" I believed my husband every single time he would tell me I was worthless. I felt like nothing."

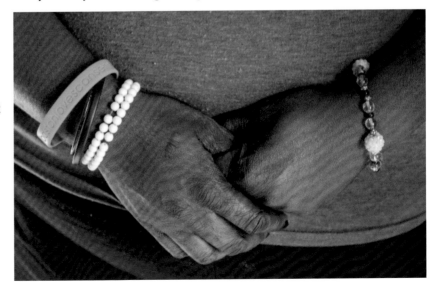

BRENDA, 48
BOSTON, MA

There is a notable disparity between homeless perceptions and reality. While the general public identifies addiction (85%) and mental illness (67%) each as a primary cause of homelessness, only 26% of homeless people suffer from a mental illness, and 33% suffer from an addiction, some of whom fall into both categories.[4,45]

"I was first just friends with my husband when he came out of jail. I knew better, and he just used me to look like he was living the married family life to look good while he was on probation. I was just a stepping stone. A year ago, I had knee replacement surgery and became sick after developing a blood clot. At this time, my marriage was rocky at best. My husband was staying up on his phone until three in the morning. I told him, 'If you don't tell me what's going on, I'm going to call the phone company and find out.' He put his fist through the wall, his hand on my throat, and tried to hit me with an iron.

I had a nervous breakdown. I've never felt anything like it. I called my best friend and told her that I felt like I was going to hurt myself. An ambulance picked me up, and I found myself in a mental hospital for nineteen days. Meanwhile, my husband hit me with a restraining order and emptied out the apartment. He took my phone, my computer, overdrew my bank account by $500, and took my kids' birth certificates. The landlord thought I was dead but eventually found me staying at my sister's. Our apartment had been torn apart, and there were holes in the walls and lights ripped out of place. It was a mess."

> **"People need to hear about this; we don't all have the same story. None of us belong here."**

"One day my sister asks if I have checked his Facebook. He had put himself 'In A Relationship' with my best friend, the one who had called the ambulance. I had another breakdown. It's not every day that you get abandoned. Looking back on it, I realize they had that going on for a while. She was a psychiatric nurse and my husband, and I would go to her for help after his mother died, and he was contemplating suicide. She

been my best friend for forty years and was supposedly giving him counseling lessons upstairs as I waited down below and apparently that's not what was happening. But I wrote her a letter telling her I forgive her. Not for her, but for me, and I wished them luck. I was devastated, but now I am a lot better off, even though I am in a shelter. I'm doing this on my own. I am starting from scratch. I can look in the mirror and know that I am a good person. I'm standing up for myself now, and I'm happy."

"Since I have been here, I have seen a whole new world. I don't think I was ignorant of homelessness, but I was ignorant of the multitude of homeless people and the multitude of people here with a mental disease. There aren't enough places for them, so they bring them in, throw some prescriptions at them, and toss them back in the street. A person who has schizophrenia or something like that, they're dealing with a slow car crash minute after minute, day after day. You don't understand when a person has a mental illness. That's why they're taking drugs: they're trying to self-medicate. I've seen my sister. My sister was a heroin addict before they diagnosed her when she was a teenager. People need to hear about this; we don't all have the same story. None of us belong here."

39

ANONYMOUS
BOSTON, MA

"I really shouldn't be here, but then again none of us should, right? I gave up my apartment to be with my husband before he died. When he passed, I wasn't on the lease and had to find something else. I got tired of couch surfing and using my friends and family, so eventually, I finally decided to hold my head high and walk through these shelter doors. I swallowed my pride and did what I had to do. Little things happen day by day, and gradually things are getting better.

My husband died of kidney failure. He had kidney failure for ten years, and we really didn't see the symptoms until he was too far gone. It hit him so hard, and he just wanted to go. I knew what to expect and knew it was coming. One day I came home, and he just wasn't there anymore. We'd gone to the clinic, and he was feeling fine, we were talking all about how we were going to have me put on the lease, but he passed before we could get to it."

"I have three children who know about my situation but I'm not going to let myself depend on them. I've been here for over a year and have been waiting for apartment approval for the last six months. This way of living is a struggle for now, but I have a job right now and have a second one set up for when I move into my apartment. The stability of this shelter has helped me find my strength and motivated me to get involved in the city's homeless issue. Now I work for the Boston's Council on Housing and Homelessness. I was put on disability in 2006, so this job has really renewed my belief that I can still learn, and I can still help others."

> " **The stability of this shelter has helped me find my strength and motivated me to get involved in the city's homeless issue.** "

Because people who lack stable housing may require additional public services, such as crisis centers, emergency services, and detoxification services, multiple studies have found long-term shelters and housing programs to be a cheaper alternative (~$12,800 vs. ~$35,580 annually).[17,43,54]

"Suddenly I'm in Boston's City Hall talking to the mayor about homelessness and having my voice heard. I used to be terrified of speaking in public, and now I'm going to council meetings and speaking in front of government officials. We are still human after all. The definition of homeless only means that we are without homes. We are still human beings, and it took me a long time to realize that before I had the humility to swallow my pride and admit to myself that I was homeless. I never thought I could be this person that fights for others' rights, but here I am, working to make real progress!"

40

ANONYMOUS, 48
CLEVELAND, OH

Relationship breakdowns are a factor that attributes to homelessness up to 10% of the time. Whether it be between partners, family members, or friends, the collapse of a relationship can have devastating economic effects on an individual.[67]

"I've been homeless for the last year since my divorce. Things change, I took an early retirement because I couldn't work due to my diabetes. Once I retired, she found another man, took the kids, took the house, and now here I am. I know a lot of husbands and fathers in divorce court deserve it, but my ex-wife calculated this one. I paid for the house her new man is living in for over two decades. I worked for US Airways for 25 years but can't collect my pension until I am 52. In the meantime, I am waiting on disability.

I know people that can help me, but I can't bring myself to ask anybody for something. I have dignity, and I don't want people to look at me like I'm homeless. I'm not going to stay in this situation."

"Honestly, the hesitation of a stranger's willingness to see me as a person is the hardest thing about this experience for me."

"I have three kids: 30, 22, and 18. I talk to them every day, but they don't know I'm homeless and I'd like it to stay that way. They know how I was kicked out though, and they understand what happened to me. I had my 22-year-old come up to me and say, 'Dad. I don't trust women. I love mom, but I saw what she did to you.' I told him, 'Not all women are like that. Things happen, and you can move forward from it.' She should have just told me things weren't going to work. She married a Coca Cola bottle, and now I'm a three-liter bottle, and she didn't want that. I was traveling a lot for work as well, and she didn't like that, life isn't always peaches and cream. But hey as long as my kids love me, I'm happy. I'm going to come out of this storm.

People make mistakes. You don't know what it feels like when it starts to rain, and it's cold, and you have nowhere to go. You don't know how it feels to be out here all night, and the library opens up, and you go inside to get warm and fall asleep. You can't control it because you were up all night shaking like a leaf. People don't understand when you go and sit in the train station just to get out of the elements for a minute, and then they tell you that you can't stay there. Or you go to a coffee shop to unthaw your feet, and they tell you that you can't stay there.

I feel judged by people walking through this park all the time. Honestly, the rejection by strangers to be seen as a person is the hardest thing about this experience for me. I fought for this country from 1986-1990 in the Navy. I was in Japan, Okinawa, Pearl Harbor, the Canary Islands, even Alaska. Even so, people look at me like I just murdered twenty people. How can you judge somebody you don't know? If it's the color of their skin, their religion, or their living situation, you're judging someone by, then you need to get your head out of your ass and realize you don't know a damn thing about that person. I don't' care what these people think about me. I know me."

41

KENNETH, 34
DETROIT, MI

"I started selling drugs at the age of 12. Both of my parents, all of my family, was addicted to crack or alcohol. I didn't have a lot of supervision growing up; all the adults would come over to smoke and kick the kids out to basically raise ourselves. The only lesson we were taught is that you don't come in the front room because the adults are getting high.

At the age of six, I was fending for myself and buying groceries for the house. My mother would sell our food stamps for drugs. I was carrying people's bags to their car, raking leaves, shoveling snow, cleaning houses, you name it- whatever I had to do to get a meal.

My father died when I was nine, and that's when my mother decided to get clean to raise me. By then, I already felt grown up. I didn't want to listen to my mom! Because of her, I was eating out of a garbage can during lunch at my school. Because of her, my friends would throw chips on the ground to watch me eat it because they knew how hungry I was.

When I was in elementary school, I started selling candy to my classmates. Other kids were doing this too, so I would put laundry ticket numbers in the bags I sold. At lunchtime, if you had the same number as me, you would get a free dollar bag of candy. So, then everyone would come and buy their candy from me. I was doing that at like seven years old. So that hustler mentality has always been there.

As a 12-year-old, my friend and I pulled together what little allowance we had and bought some dope. We set up shop on a street corner in Detroit and started selling. We bought a gun for 50 bucks- you need a weapon, or you are just going to get robbed for your dope. It's hard for me to look at my 11-year-old son and think that when I was his age, I was selling sacks of drugs on the street corner with a gun in my back pocket.

I got kicked out of school at 14 and just continued to sell after that. That was all well and good until I decided to try my own product. People will always ask, 'You see what this is doing to you, why would you use crack cocaine?' Well, it wasn't like that. Sure, some of my customers were living in attics or abandoned buildings, but some of them pulled up in Cadillacs decked in jewelry with a beautiful wife beside them. I didn't think this would crush me and destroy my life, but that's when I dropped off the edge.

I kept my appearance up for a long time, but after two years I started looking more and more like an addict. I took my GED long before I got clean. I did so well on the GED that the program I was in paid for my college. So, I attended Baker College, where I met the mother of my children when I was 22. I would get high during the week and come back and cram for my exams and test on Thursday. I graduated from Jobs Corps and from Baker College with a degree in Information Systems Technology with a 3.2 GPA, higher than a kite.

I knew I wasn't ready to be in the world still, but I went back and forth from Detroit and Flint a lot to see the mother of my children and my newborn baby. My addiction progressively got worse, and I screwed over a lot of people in Flint- my family, my friends, my children.

Eventually, I moved to Detroit, and I just got stuck there. It takes a powerful disease to leave an air-conditioned house with big screen TVs to go squat in an abandoned home where you shit in a bucket. The house I was staying in was only a fourth of a home; the rest had been burned to the ground. It was a smoker's home; if you came early enough in the day, then you got a place to sleep. Drugs can take you to an animal level, and this was definitely an animal level.

This is where I begin to get paranoid and strung out. I start to think I am being watched by the mafia."

"I got lost in my head one day and went on a walk. I was leaving paper trails behind me like Hansel and Gretel. I was scared and lost at one point, so I went into a police station for help. I'm there just screaming as loud as I can, 'Please please help me!', and they send me to a mental hospital. The next day, I checked myself out and have my mom pick me up and take me back to her home. When she gets back from running errands, I'm in her home telling her to whisper because 'They can hear us.'

She starts crying and throws me into the car to take me back to a hospital. When we pulled over at a gas station, I smash two bottles together and hold them to my neck like I'm going to stab myself. I think I was actually going to until this guy comes and tackles me to the ground, saving my life. I was gone, just checked out, punching my own ticket.

Despite recent drops in the national poverty rate (12.3%), Detroit's poverty rate sits at a remarkable 35.7%, with the child poverty rate at 48%.[11,26]

Then I took my medication, I talked to the right people, and bit by bit I'm pulling myself back together. Some people never come back from that, so I'm blessed. I did all these things, but I never did love myself enough to keep myself from getting high. My complete focus in treatment now is learning how to love Kenneth. You can't love yourself if all you do is self-sabotage. I can actually say that I love myself today, and that's a step I thought I would never take."

"Poetry is where I found love for myself. I'm focusing on Ken right now, not becoming a star or anything. But I was born to be successful, and I've just been running from that.

We have a poetry class here, and I started writing poems. The teacher loved them and invited me to perform at a few benefits he does. The poem I recited is called "Ants In My Pants." When I have thoughts about using, I just tell myself that people at the performing hall and people on the soundboard don't get high. I still think about using, I mean I've been using since I was 10 years old. But I don't get high anymore, I just go about my day."

> **"At the age of six, I was fending for myself and buying groceries for the house."**

"Ants in My Pants"

I get up just to get down
It would take the combined strength of Hercules and Samson to restrain me
See I'm a mover, I'm a shaker, I'm a wheeler, I'm a dealer, I'm a stealer
I'm the best, the buster, the car, the train, the plane
I get down just to get up
It would take the heel of God's shoe just to stop my ascension
See I'm a riser, I'm a flyer, I'm a propeller, I'm an excellor, I'm a soar, I'm a roar, I'm Mufasa.
The king, the lion, the star, the leaf
I get up just to get through,
It would take the tribe of Zubu and ten Shakas to cease my invasion
See I'm a virus, I'm a destroyer, I'm a foyer, I'm a hire, I'm a fire, I'm a mother fucker
I'm a run a mucker, I'm an ignis, I'm a sickness, I'm a disease, I'm AIDS
The plan, the solution, the answer, the cure
I get down just to get by
It would take the shift of the nation to stop my rotation
See I'm a creator I'm an agitator, I'm an irrigator, I'm a grower, I'm a knower,
I'm a laser, I'm a stargazer, I'm Orion,
The belt, the strap, the whip, the extension cord
Oh shit mama, please not the extension cord
For over 400 years I've been beaten into submission
But I won't stop moving forward
Because I got ants in my pants

42

JANET, 57
CHICAGO, IL

People aged 41–60 make up the largest population of Chicago's homeless, with 30% of all sheltered individuals and 47% of all unsheltered individuals living within the age range.[53]

"I became homeless about five years ago. It began when I was fired at the laundromat I worked at, where both my age and hearing were at fault. I was told by management that I was ignoring customers. Well, in reality, I just couldn't hear them! There are about thirty machines spinning at a time, so I just couldn't hear people trying to get my attention.

I had a lot of trouble finding a job after that. I had worked there for twenty years and didn't even know how to make a resume. Who knew you would need a resume for a laundry job at a nursing home? So after I ran out of unemployment, I began going through my savings. I was able to survive like that for a year and a half actually before eventually having my home foreclosed on. It's as simple as that."

"I was staying at a large shelter for a few months until I developed pneumonia. I went into the doctor and was told I had a blood clot in my lung as well. If I had not have gone to the doctor, I would have died that month. After being recommended to find a smaller shelter, I finally got into this place. In seven months, they helped me back on my feet and find a place, so now I volunteer here a few times a week.

"I went to the doctor and was told I had a blot clot in my lung. I almost died."

I no longer need to find work after I received disability for my bipolar depression. I always felt a little unstable emotionally but never thought I would have a term for it. I was going from these extreme highs to extreme lows, especially when I was unemployed. I was so stressed that I wasn't paying any attention to my mental health and once I got sick it started happening more often. I'm usually a happy person, but I would just get lost in this strange feeling of despair. It was like at times nothing mattered to me. That sort of apathy for yourself is a bizarre feeling; it's like you don't want to be you or even care to. Now I'm talking about a dozen pills a day, going to a support group, and seeing a therapist. Since then, I have also had my hearing corrected, and that has helped my anxiety more than you know."

"When you are struggling, there really are a lot of places that can help and people who want to help. The problem is a lot of people living in the streets are stuck in certain situations where they can't be accommodated. Since I've volunteered here, I've talked with mothers who don't want to go to shelters and split up their families. I've spoken to veterans who suffer from PTSD and can't handle being around so many people, and you can't blame them for that. To be accepted in a lot of these helping programs you need to somewhat fit the profile they are looking for and, unfortunately, many people just don't."

43

CASSIE, 40
CHICAGO, IL

"I became homeless through my struggle with addiction. It all started around the time my dad died from elective surgery. I had four teeth pulled right before I delivered his eulogy. The painkillers they gave me for that were just the start. Soon after this, I began to use just to numb myself from life.

At the time my dad had just passed away, I was raising a kid with bipolar disorder, and was with a husband who was apathetic and hopelessly depressed. I began stealing my mom's MS medication to feed my addiction. It got to a point where I was taking 30 a day. She brought charges against me, and I was convicted of a felony. After prison I went to a mental institution, then rehab, then I didn't have anywhere to go. Withdrawals almost killed me. I couldn't sit, stand, or even really breathe. It's the worst pain I can possibly imagine; your bones cry out in pain, and your skin feels like it's crawling off your body."

"I don't blame my mom for what she did; I had loving parents. They adopted my brother and I when I was just one, and my brother was six. Before we were adopted, we were in very abusive situations. When my (eventual) foster parents would visit us, they would find cigarette burns and dark marks all over my brother. He took beatings for me and probably saved my life, but because of how badly he was abused, he is now mentally disabled and has stayed in a mental institution for his adult life."

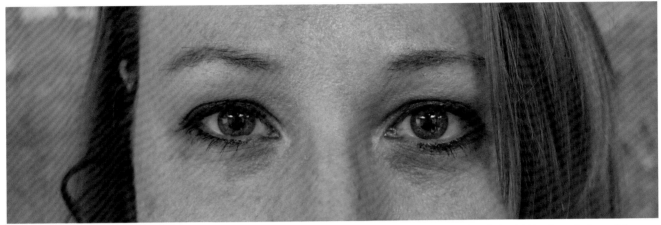

In Chicago, 23% of women staying in shelters have been previously incarcerated, while 58% of unsheltered homeless women have been formerly incarcerated.[12]

"My husband killed himself when I was in prison. He tried to commit suicide four times before he succeeded. On a Monday morning, they found him dead on someone's front lawn. We were both diabetic, and they found two empty bottles of insulin on him. I don't know what to call that feeling of dread, but I knew he was dead before they even told me. I try not to think about that time in my life now.

I first met my husband in church when I was a kid. Four years ago, we reconnected and got married right away. We didn't even make it two years. He suffered from severe depression and was just lost in life. His first suicide attempt was right in front of me.

"My husband killed himself when I was in prison. He tried four times before he succeeded."

He walked into the kitchen, grabbed a knife, and slit his wrists open. At first, I couldn't move, I just stared in horror for a second and watched the blood drip down his hand. What pain must you be going through to want to end your life so urgently? And right in front of your wife?"

"One of the hardest things about being homeless is walking past houses with families living in them and seeing smiling faces. I just wish people would understand that we don't all pick this life. I didn't start out when I was ten years old thinking I wanted to be a criminal, an addict, and be homeless on top of it. Life happens. With the struggles I've faced, maintaining self-control through it all just felt impossible. You have to learn to accept it and get on with it. This isn't going to stop me. It's a bump in the road, but it's not going to stop me."

44

JONATHAN, 56
ST. LOUIS, MO

"I've been homeless many times. I was homeless after I lost my mother, and again after I lost my wife. It pains me to say it, but I lost my home to drugs, dope to be honest with you. I would feel so lost and hopeless, I just didn't have any reason to keep moving, and all I wanted to do was feel numb. What do you do when your reason to live dies? How do you cope with that? At the time I thought it didn't even matter if I stayed here or not. I just didn't care about myself for a long time.

I have mouth cancer from smoking, and I now have rheumatoid arthritis. I'm old and struggling, and at this point, people can barely hear me when I'm talking to them. When you're homeless, people don't want to listen to you, but as my cancer worsens people can't hear me anyways. I've got a young man willing to talk to me right now, but you don't know how hard it is for me to pronounce my words so you can even understand me. Sometimes I feel like God made the perfect storm for me then forgot about letting the sun shine through the clouds. This is just the way things shake out for some people."

"I've been out here for three or four months now. I've sobered up, and I'm getting my mind back a little bit by staying at a day shelter. I'm staying positive- I'm still smiling, aren't I? Who said you need all your teeth to smile? The sun is out today, there aren't any clouds in sight, and I have an appointment this week to see if I qualify for disability and can get my train back on the tracks. I don't know what you are thinking, but I think I look pretty damn disabled. At the same time, what can I do right now? I don't see the worth in sulking anymore. I just want to get out of my current situation before the winter sets in.

> ## " Sometimes I feel like God made the perfect storm for me then forgot about letting the sun shine through the clouds. "

You always have to wonder how this happened and how you got to this point. You can't keep your youth young man, and you can never keep the people around you as long as you like. Treasure others, treasure your youth, and treasure your joints! Someday it will hurt to walk, and that day will be a day too soon."

Although the number of chronically homeless individuals increased by 2% between 2017 to 2018, the count has dropped 26% since 2007 due to various long-term housing programs.[13]

45

LYNN, 53
KANSAS CITY, MO

An estimated 13% of the homeless population is employed. However, of the 3,007 counties in the United States, there are only 22 where an individual can afford a single bedroom apartment on federal minimum wage.[27,64]

"I've been out here for two months but only needed a day to see how differently I'm treated for being homeless. I don't really care about what people think about me. They aren't better than me for judging me for being homeless, and I'm no better than them.

I had a falling out with my roommate. I was working, and he was an alcoholic. Don't get me wrong, I love a beer or two, but I can't handle being around someone downing a case a night. I don't want that drama anymore, I don't want to fight or anything like that, I just want my life together and to move forward. I want to live near the library. I plan on reading and learning as often as I can. I'm just interested in bettering myself as a person. There is no use trying to find housing if I am not willing to better myself as a person first because if I don't do that, I'll find myself back here."

"I work for a temp company, so I'll do whatever they need me to. Construction, filing papers, day labor- you name it. I'm a hard worker and a loyal employee, but I have made some mistakes. I've snorted this and smoked that. I wouldn't say I have ever had an addiction, but at a certain point, there's only so 'high' you can be. At a certain point, you need to come down. I realized that and backed away from that lifestyle. I would say that's one of the better decisions I have made in life: backing down from something I knew wasn't good for me before it ruined who I was. I'm a religious man. We all live in sin. When I make mistakes, I try to learn from it and not fall back into old traps."

"I hope I'm not the only person you run into with future goals, who is just looking to get back on their feet. I'm nothing special. I meet people like myself more often than not at the shelter: people wanting to move forward in life. Homeless people are rarely who we take them to be."

46

TRACY, 60
DENVER, CO

"I live on social security. When you live on social security, finding housing can be a nightmare. I was living in a basement for a little while, but that didn't work out. Soon enough, I find myself living on the streets. I lived at the civic center park for a year. I had a couple of young guys who were my protectors basically. They didn't sleep far from me at night and made sure I was okay during the day. The winter was the harsh part. It was cold, wet, and brutal. I've now been here for about a year and a half. I may be able to go to a senior center and hope to get a lottery pick for housing, but it is usually around an eight-year wait.

I had the stroke in 2010 the day after my birthday. Luckily, the only thing the stroke affected was the grip in my right hand, and sometimes I just won't be able to speak out the words in my head. I had my stroke while I had cancer. I had to have surgery soon after to remove a tumor. I am cancer free now with no signs of spread- blood count normal. A week after I had that surgery, my wife passed away from heart problems. We were together for over 26 years. It was a rough year. Her name was Donna. She was 52."

"I don't drink. I don't smoke. I don't do drugs and never have, but people still treat me like that just because I'm homeless. I went to a hospital, and the doctor insisted that I get tested for HIV and a series of diseases just because of my housing situation."

"There are people all around me, and I'm still alone. This isn't home for me."

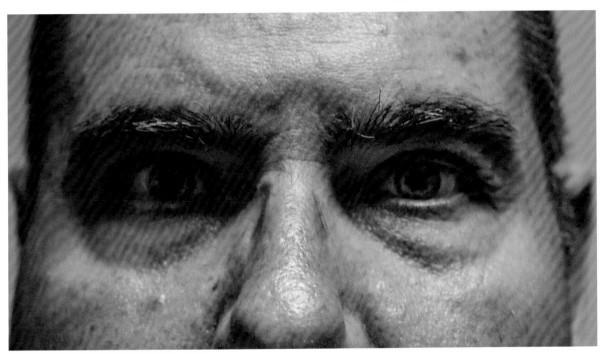

23% of all home renters in Colorado cannot afford the home they are in now and are at risk of becoming homeless. Due to the increase in population and subsequent increase in housing costs, nearly one-fourth of Denver residents spend at least half of their income on rent.[6,9]

"I wasn't really sure how I was going to handle it when I became homeless, but my upbringing taught me that no matter the situation, you gut it out and work through it and that's what I'm doing. Some people here get caught in the idea where all they care to be is homeless because they adopt the way society treats them. That's not me. I'm living in a shelter and consider myself homeless because I'm still not home.

The hardest thing about being homeless? Not having a place of my own. Companionship. There are people all around me, and I'm still alone. This isn't home for me. There's not much to me that is a worse feeling than that. I never thought I would be homeless. I never thought homelessness was this big of an issue until I found myself a part of it. I never looked down on homeless people. I would just let them be. When I am on the other side of things, it's fascinating how people seem to go out of their way to ignore me. One paycheck- that's all it takes to end up where I am. I used to be a reserve firefighter.

I would encourage people to be more compassionate. Don't be so self-centered. Everybody walks this planet, and we need to share it. No one is really better or worse than anybody else. It's all temporary."

47

ANDRE, 51
DENVER, CO

"The fact that I am on disability is a major factor as to why I am not able to find a place. When you are on disability, you are only allowed to earn a certain amount a month; it varies for each individual. When you get close to that amount, you have to stop working or risk losing your disability. So, with each month, you fall more and more behind. That's why so many people you see out here are elderly, on walkers, or in a wheelchair. For whatever reason, they got behind in their bills, and sooner or later they were evicted. In the Denver area, it is incredibly difficult to find affordable housing, and any available house is gone as soon as it is made available.

If you do find places you can afford, you're still in trouble. I find it that people are reluctant to rent to people on disability. Renters might believe that people on disability might be hanging around bad crowds or might not be able to keep up on their rent. It's a stereotype; you wouldn't even recognize most people on disability. They base their opinions on the one in the crowd who fits the stereotype and treats everyone else in the group as if they are that outlier."

"I was diagnosed with HIV in '94 and AIDS in '05. To be honest, I am more concerned about living homeless than I am about living with AIDS. You don't have to die as soon now as you used to. I've been through cancer as well, and that had a better chance of taking me out than AIDS. I had three cancer growths in my right atrium and went through eight months of chemo. Doctors believed the cancer was likely caused by a combination of my AIDS medications. The chemo eradicated the cancer, and now the AIDS is something I just work with and take day by day."

> **"To be honest, I am more concerned about living homeless than I am about living with AIDS."**

The average annual cost of healthcare for HIV is an estimated $39,000. As a result, studies conducted in major cities have found that up to 50% of people living with HIV/AIDS are at risk of becoming homeless.[33,48]

"I didn't plan on being homeless. No one does. Where I grew up was considered the ghetto and is now suburban. Nobody used to want to be there. Now it's a haven and expensive for everyone who doesn't already own a home. The cost of rent out here is just going through the roof, and when my landlord raised the rent, we weren't able to keep up.

I came here for about five months and moved into the housing program they have here. You really can't plan a life when you don't have a place to plan a life. You can't prioritize your life when you don't know where you will be every two months."

48

ALLAN, 59
BOISE, ID

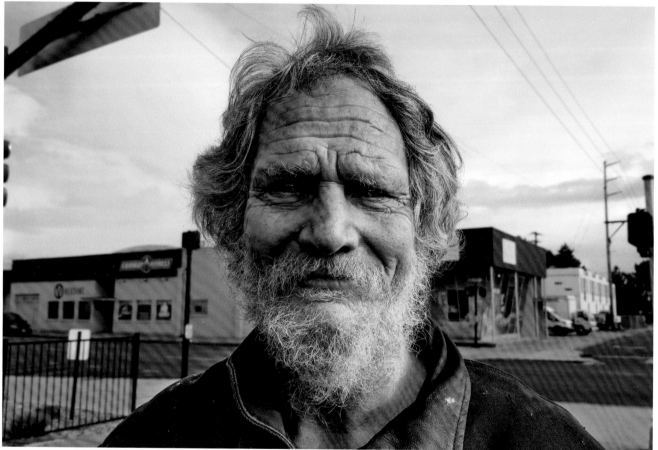

Schizophrenics living with depression face a great risk of suicidal behavior. An incredible 20% of schizophrenics attempt suicide with approximately 5%-6% succeeding.[61,62]

"I was homeless for three years until I was able to get my social security. The social security is what keeps me off the streets, but after bills and rent I only have about $30 to spend a month, so I have to sit out here and beg. I have a few mental conditions that keep me from being able to hold a job.

I have schizophrenia. I'll get severe paranoia and will have no idea why I'm scared. It's always been a problem for me in public places, like a supermarket. I was having problems being around people in the shelters with my mental condition. I can't sleep when there is someone else near me, and I can't think. That doesn't mean I'm stupid, I know I have issues with my mental health, but there's nothing I can really do about it. I'm on medication which has been a great help, but that doesn't mean that I'm sane necessarily."

"Truthfully, I was sexually abused when I was very small. I was born a hermaphrodite and sold to a brothel. I suffered a lot of abuse there, and it's taken me a really long time to get through it. When I was 18, I was shot in the head at Ann Morrison Park. You can see the little scar on my forehead where they saved my life and were able to give me plastic surgery. The bullet went through the center of my mind and left me with brain damage. Living life has been very hard for me since then.

I'm not stupid; I used to be an incredible piano player. I was always sharp. After I got shot, I had amnesia and became relatively dumb for a long time. I had

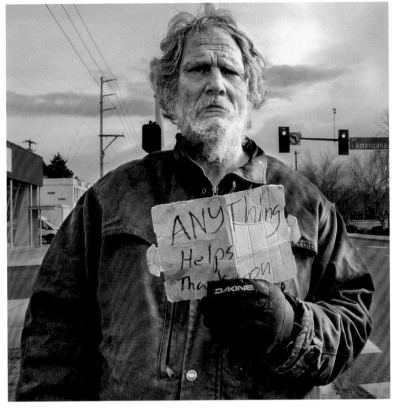

severe amnesia and couldn't hold a conversation for about ten years. Eventually, I remembered the years that I forgot. I would see a picture of myself, and it would take me a second, but I would recognize myself. I would completely forget I ever got shot. It was a really surreal experience for me, but I'm very thankful to have my mind back, therapy helped me a lot."

"There are always voices and conversations going on in my head that I can't control."

"Eventually, I was able to hold down a job as a mechanic but started having problems with paranoia, even delusional types of paranoia. This was about ten years ago when I started getting signs of schizophrenia. There are always voices and conversations going on in my head that I can't control. After that, I sort of got stuck with severe depression. My depression was caused by certain life situations from my childhood, like abuse. I'm on medication that really helps me with the depression. I stopped crying on an everyday basis. I was clinically depressed before, and it's really subsided now.

I have a dual-personality disorder as well, but that only comes out when I get really scared or provoked. I will just get terrified and blackout. It's frightening not to know who you are for a period of time. I've had friends just tell me I'll act really strange and paranoid, but this doesn't often happen anymore. I started doing this when I was a child because I suffered from abuse, and it was my way of dealing with it."

49

JAMES, 62
BOISE, ID

Idaho is one of the cheapest states to live in the United States, with the average rent for a one bedroom apartment being $810. Despite this, a full-time worker living on minimum wage would have less than $450 a month to spend on additional living expenses, like groceries, electricity, and healthcare.[16]

"I've been homeless for about four years. I moved up to Boise after the divorce and met a lovely lady. We lived together for almost two decades. On year 18, she had a stroke. When she was in the hospital getting it treated, they found tumors in her brain, and she died a few months later in my arms.

After that, I had nothing but myself. I really struggled for a long time to keep going, to keep my two dogs. When I lost my job, everything fell apart. I was living in a motel week by week, and once I got canned, I couldn't come up with rent money and out I went. I had to get rid of my dogs and was left by myself entirely."

"The loneliness really gets to me now. I miss her every day, even though it's been four years. I still think about her all the time. It's tough to cope with it. Some days I don't cope with it. I just sit there doing nothing all day and get absorbed in it. It has gotten easier with time. The first couple of years were really hard. We did everything together. It was hard, especially the way she passed away. She didn't look like herself; she was so pale and skinny."

> **"I miss her every day, even though it's been four years. I still think about her all the time."**

"I'm on the verge of retiring in four months. I worked my whole life since I was 16. I have only been out of work for the last few years since I have been homeless, but nobody will hire me at this age, especially if you are homeless. In July, I won't get my full benefits, but I will get around 80% of it, which should be about $1000 a month, and that is enough for me. I had a lady come over to me in the apartments who offered me a place to stay once I start getting my pension. I am incredibly grateful for that."

"When people do give, I thank them as many times as I can before they drive off. The old lady and I used to stop and give homeless people money or food when we came to the store. My wife and I would provide them with a box of food. I always felt sorry for them like everyone else does. I never thought I would be out here. Even though we were generous, I still always thought they were alcoholics or drug attics. A lot of homeless people are, but a lot of them aren't, and I was wrong about that. I don't blame people for thinking that, there are a lot of people who only ask for money for beer or liquor. You don't know what people are doing, but if someone has cynical thoughts when they see me, I take no offense."

50

RAYMOND, 67
SPOKANE, WA

Injection users of substances like cocaine, crack, and methamphetamine are over 25 times more likely to have the hepatitis C virus than those who do not inject.[50]

"It's easy to fall into this web, but it's a lot harder to get out of it. I was a certified nursing assistant, and later a physical therapist assistant. I was working at hospice care for years before I was let go after being unable to keep up with my workload. I was getting overwhelmed when I was getting interferon treatment for my hepatitis C. I was living in this fog for about six months, where I didn't know what was up or down. I don't think I was dying, but the treatment certainly made me feel like it. This was right after I bought a home. My home was foreclosed on soon after, and that left me without a place to stay.

I've had hepititis C since 1986. There is a sort of cure, where I was injecting myself with medicine every week, but the injection site on my stomach kept blistering, and I'd have to keep circling out wider and wider. I felt it wasn't working as it should and started drinking because at the time I was very depressed.

Because of my alcohol use, I was kicked off the plan due to my own neglect. I can't knock myself for it now. It's a new adventure every day. I walk outside and praise God for what I have, I smell the roses, and I take it one step at a time."

"I'm on social security now earning about $1200 a month. Because I never paid off my student loans from the 1970s, I now owe $138,000 in student debt. If you learn only one thing from this talk with me, remember to pay off your student loans! After my loans are paid off, I'm left with just under $1,000 a month. I'm saving that up to move out this summer when my finances are all in order."

"I cannot express to you how appreciative I am of the services that have been provided for me. I am on Medicaid and Medicare. I have a membership at the senior center, where I can meet friends and get food. Maybe I don't have everything, but I am forever grateful knowing I still have more than others less fortunate.

> "Maybe I don't have everything, but I am forever grateful knowing I still have more than others less fortunate."

Homeless people will get slammed and ridiculed for things that aren't based on homelessness. It's the drug addicts in our homeless society that don't respect themselves or others that do so much damage to homelessness. At the senior center, I hear people talking about how the homeless folk ruined the bathrooms or damaged the walls. They have no idea I'm homeless, but sometimes I wish they did. I treat everything and everyone there with the utmost respect. I feel like I owe it to the center; they feed me after all!"

51

[YOUR NAME HERE]

[INSERT PHOTO HERE]

The final question I asked in each interview was this: "If you could say one thing to society about the homeless experience, what would it be?".

Nearly every answer I received can be summed up with the sentiment: "We are all people, and it can happen to you." The original goal for Fifty Sandwiches was not to present the diversity of homelessness. This only came to be after realizing just how many people are introduced to the unexpected.

Many Americans live paycheck to paycheck, with 40% of adults being unable to afford an unexpected $400 expense.[19] Many of us may be just a medical bill, a natural disaster, a lawsuit, or a job loss away from finding ourselves in the same shoes as the struggling stranger we walk past on the street. This profile aims to demonstrate the grim but important reminder of the thin line separating your story and the stories presented in this book. Nobody starts here.

Merely understanding that each person you walk by on a given day has a lifetime of experiences, stories, and struggles just as complex as your own is the key to humanizing the homeless.

If this book can make someone turn their head when they pass a homeless person, then Fifty Sandwiches has served its purpose. When you turn your head, you are deliberately giving your preconceived notions a second thought. The greatest adversity homelessness faces is ignorance; not being taken seriously as a real crisis in our country. If I can turn your head, then I can force you to acknowledge that person's existence and their struggles. After that, it's up to you. What do you want to do about that feeling? I can't force you to empathize or help- all I've done is take away your denial.

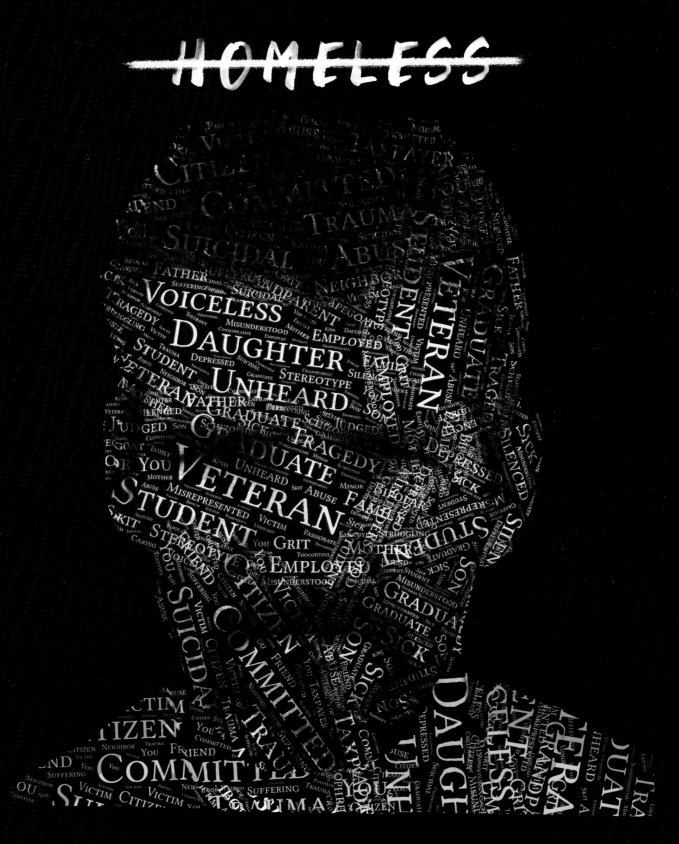

Often referring to himself in the third person, Justin Wilder Doering is the author and creator of Fifty Sandwiches. A native of Coeur d'Alene, Idaho, Doering graduated from Boise State University with...

Look-

I rewrote the Author's Biography about a dozen times before finally settling on free-form thought. I was going to piece together a humorous bio filled with crap you can find online but let me use this opportunity to give my own interview: an account of this project from my perspective. I can't write some clichè, censored biography of accolades and accomplishments here thinking readers will laud me for writing a book filled to the brim with the hardships of others. How am I supposed to create a book based on the struggles of homeless people and expect it to be acceptable that I do not share my own?

In fact, the very idea of an Author's Biography comes to me as a moral dilemma, where I am forced to weigh ego and hypocrisy, where my name on the spine sends chills up my own. After all, this project shouldn't be about me- it's not. Fifty Sandwiches was funded by others and built on the stories of others, yet it has been my name you see in articles and my face you see in interviews. If there's one thing I learned from my interviews, it's that it's always better to overshare to be understood than be overlooked because you're scared of being looked over.

This project has forced me to face guilt and self-doubt, equipped with only a vague understanding of which of my actions are truly genuine. I struggle with depression, and I settle for anxiety. I've questioned my ability to see this project through, and I've questioned my true intentions with its purpose. For over three months, I drove my van down the middle of a road balanced somewhere between exploitation and journalism. This isn't some project with steadfast conviction. The only aspects of Fifty Sandwiches that have not been met with apprehension are that America's homeless are in desperate need of a platform to be heard and understood, and that I do not know what I am doing.

I won't walk you through my failures and obstacles, but this was not easy- though I've been told few things worth doing are. This entire process has been a learning experience as I attempt to transform a rudimentary skill set into a well-executed book. That means accepting that a lot of my efforts will go unnoticed, but those that don't yield a direct return are another notch in the belt towards the next effort. I don't have an agent, a designer, a publisher, or an editor. If I did, it wouldn't have taken ~~two~~ three years to publish.

But here we are. This idea sprouted in my head when I was 15 and spent a decade sharpening its nails and scratching at my conscious. To let it out, to see it come together, is surreal.

Thank you for reading and thank you for being a part of this journey.

FUTURE OF FIFTY SANDWICHES

MORE THAN A BOOK

This is a project involving more than just myself and the incredible people who donated to make the journey happen. For many, it takes great humility to be able to surrender your convictions and adopt a new-found perspective based on truth. With your help, Fifty Sandwiches can be a living, breathing movement that can affect society on a grander scale than I had ever planned.

SPEAKING

In an effort to spread the word of Fifty Sandwiches and effectively humanize the homeless, I've spoken with community members, students, and teachers alike. The objective of these speaking opportunities is to present listeners with a foundation of understanding built upon Fifty Sandwiches' journey, purpose, and stories.

Fifty Sandwiches is always in search of new avenues to share its message. If you have an opportunity where you believe Fifty Sandwiches can make a lasting impact in the minds of others, please do not hesitate to contact Info@FiftySandwiches.com.

Looking as if he just rolled out of a van, Justin Doering discusses Fifty Sandwiches on Great Day Washington.

Speaking at The Center for The Homeless Annual Luncheon, Justin Doering shares the stories and mission behind Fifty Sandwiches to an audience in South Bend, IN. Photo taken by Ryan Glasky.

#FiftySandwiches Challenge

Our unwillingness to recognize the depth and complexities of people living without homes leaves us with a close-minded view of the homeless crisis in the United States. With the original intent of widening the perspectives of its readers, Fifty Sandwiches has evolved with a new plan to encourage those very readers to take the reins and conduct their own interviews.

Fifty Sandwiches' readers- people like you- can step out of your comfort zone and become an active part of correcting society's lens on your own accord. Whether you're a teacher, a student, or an active citizen, foster open discussions, share stories, and urge others to do the same. Someone's story you capture just might give someone else the confidence and interest to go conduct their own interview, and so forth.

The goal is to create a whole movement of engaged citizens posting interviews from shelters with the #FiftySandwiches hashtag to share the stories of those they meet and spread awareness. By presenting the experiences and realities of homelessness within your network and community, your efforts can make a lasting impact on society's outlook and subsequent handling of the issue. With your help, the purpose of this book can become wholly obsolete and someday, Fifty Sandwiches will be seen as an archaic reminder of how things once were.

Soon enough, this could develop into a whole generation of people who see the homeless as they should be seen: as people. A generation of people who can empathize with the struggles of others to the extent where it encourages them to better themselves. A generation of people whose motivations for self-improvement involve improving the lives of others. It may sound idealistic, but you don't make significant changes on little ideas.

Conducting Your Own Interviews

Becoming a Fifty Sandwiches volunteer by conducting your own interviews can be a gratifying experience for both you and the individual experiencing homelessness. While the interviewee is given a rare chance to share their story and be heard, you get a first-hand opportunity to gain valuable insight into the personal experiences, struggles, and causes of homelessness.

You Will Need

 1 Local Shelter's Contact Information

2 Smartphone or Camera

3 Recording Device or App

Reaching Out

For safety purposes, do not approach strangers on the street. Instead, reach out to local shelters in your area to let them know about the project and your interest in interviewing some of their residents. It's important to remember to respect the privacy of both the people working in the shelter as well as the residents. Be sure you have full permission from the shelter and the interviewee to record the discussion and photograph the subject before proceeding forward with an interview. If they do not wish to be photographed, do not fret! 'Anonymous' interviews can be just as heartfelt and eye-opening.

Always remember that these people are in the midst of facing incredible hardships; empathy and understanding on your behalf are absolutely essential!

Interview Process

After getting their consent, turn on your recording device and get their name, age, and location. These discussions can be a nerve-wracking, emotional process for both parties. After all, your goal is to encourage people in great distress to open up about their outstanding struggles to a complete stranger. Some people are more than happy to share while others may be more reserved. You need to be willing to dive outside of your comfort zone while being careful not to force them to leave theirs. Be mindful of your body language and eye contact. Provide them your undivided attention. They deserve it.

A list of questions is helpful, but not required. The goal is to use their answers as jumping off points to guide the direction of discussion. Look for the story behind the philosophy and the philosophy behind the story, always. Focus on building a bond and never be afraid to ask the tough questions and dig deep.

Justin interviews Eva at a park in Tallahassee. Photo by WCTV News.

QUESTIONS TO CONSIDER

1. How long have you been homeless?
2. How did you end up homeless?
3. What is your greatest struggle in life right now?
4. How has your experience changed your perception of homelessness?
5. How would you say society sees homelessness?
6. If you could tell society one thing about the homeless experience what would it be?

Snap a few photos from varying angles when the interview is complete. Thank them for their time and demonstrate your full appreciation for telling their story. Just because life's hardships are essential to discuss, doesn't mean they are easy to share.

When you are back home, transcribe the recorded interview and remove filler content that you feel takes away from the story. Be careful when paraphrasing to maintain accuracy and avoid reframing the context of their words!

SUBMISSION

There are three different options for you to submit your interview to be published on the Fifty Sandwiches website and social platforms:

1 (*Recommended*) Post the interview to your Instagram page with the hashtag #FiftySandwiches and tag @FiftySandwiches in the post.

2 Submit the interview at FiftySandwiches.com by clicking 'Submit Interview' and following the directions provided.

3 Email Info@FiftySandwiches.com with a copy of the transcript and photos.

Photo of a homeless man taken by Sandy Satuloff-Doering on June 16th, 1983.

During floods, ant colonies will bunch together by the thousands to form a living raft. They link arm to arm body to body on top of each other, constantly rotating and moving so no ant is in the water long enough to drown. This is an instinctual reaction. Ants live in colonies where they form hierarchies, delegate tasks, and depend on each other for their own existence. The ants cannot survive on their own or they will drown. In a society, we depend on each other. If you are not willing to get your feet wet, you can't expect someone else to do the same when you find yourself neck deep in your own storm. Clear skies today will never promise a sunny tomorrow.

Every person living on the street is not just someone we can offer to help; it is someone who is not currently a part of the raft with the rest of us. Each ant left out means the ants included in the raft have to try that much harder and be in the water that much longer to stay afloat.

Being a part of a productive society goes both ways. We move forward together, and we move backward together. Understanding homelessness is the first step towards solving the issue. Spreading awareness and seeing how their shoes fit on your feet is essential. They might be a tight fit, they might be too big, but someday they might be all you're left with when your shoes have soaked through. Whether it's your time, your money, or even your empathy, the question is **never** if you can help, but if you will.

WORKS CITED

● ●

References are also available at fiftysandwiches.com/works-cited.

1. "The 2018 Annual Homeless Assessment Report (AHAR) to Congress." The U.S. Department of Housing and Urban Development, 2018. Office of Community Planning and Development. 10 July 2018.

2. "2018 Homeless Census & Survey: Summary of Findings." Homeless Census & Survey 2018 Southern Nevada Executive Summary, Bitfocus, 2018. 9 Feb. 2018.

3. "2018 Point-In-Time Count of Persons Experiencing Homelessness in the District of Columbia." The Community Partnership for the Prevention of Homelessness, 2018. Department Of Human Services. 9 Mar. 2018.

4. "Addiction Among The Homeless Population." Sunrise House American Addiction Center, Mar. 2016, sunrisehouse.com/addiction-demographics/homeless-population/. 9 Mar. 2018.

5. Amadeo, Kimberly. "Medical Bankruptcy and the Economy." thebalance.com, the balance, 12 March 2019, https://www.thebalance.com/medical-bankruptcy-statistics-4154729. 23 Aug 2018.

6. "America's Rental Housing 2017 Interactive Tools." Joint Center For Housing Studies Of Harvard University, 2017. 19 Feb. 2018.

7. "America's Shame: 40% of Homeless Youths Are LGBT Kids." The Williams Institute, UCLA School of Law, 13 July 2012, https://williamsinstitute.law.ucla.edu/press/americas-shame-40-of-homeless-youth-are-lgbt-kids/. 20 April 2018.

8. Baker, Charlene K., and Sarah L. Cook. "Domestic Violence and Housing Problems." Socialsciences.people.hawaii.edu, Georgia State University, July 2003, socialsciences.people.hawaii.edu/publications_lib/domestic violence and housing.pdf. 10 July 2018.

9. Bennett, Michael. "2018 Colorado Housing Profile." National Low Income Housing Coalition, 2018. 7 Jan. 2018.

10. Browne, A. 1998. "Responding to the Needs of Low Income and Homeless Women Who are Survivors of Family Violence." Journal of American Medical Women's Association. 53(2): 57-64. 1 June 2018.

11. "Census: Detroit Income Rises, Poverty Rate Doesn't Improve." usnews.com, U.S. News, 13 Sept. 2018, https://www.usneaws.com/news/best-states/michigan/articles/2018-09-13/census-detroit-income-rises-poverty-rate-doesnt-improve. 11 Aug. 2018.

12. "Challenges to Housing Access." City of Chicago 2017 Point-in-Time Count & Survey Report, Voorhees Center for Neighborhood & Community Improvement, University of Illinois at Chicago, 2017, https://www.chicago.gov/content/dam/city/depts/fss/supp_info/Homeless/2017PITSummaryReportFinal.pdf. 30 Jan 2018.

13. "Chronically Homeless Individuals." The 2018 Annual Homeless Assessment Report (AHAR) to Congress, The U.S. Department of Housing and Urban Development, Dec. 2018, https://www.hudexchange.info/resources/documents/2018-AHAR-Part-1.pdf. 21 Jan. 2019.

14. Clow, A. and Fredhoi, C. 2006. Normalisation of salivary cortisol levels and self-report stress by a brief lunchtime visit to an art gallery by London City workers. Journal of Holistic Healthcare. 3 (2), pp. 29-32. 11 Aug. 2018.

15. Cohen, Y., et al. "Suicide among the Homeless: a 9-Year Case-Series Analysis." Abarbanel Mental Health Center, 2004. 11 Aug. 2018.

16. "Cost of Living in Boise, Idaho." Best Places, 2018, www.bestplaces.net/cost_of_living/city/idaho/boise. 10 May 2019.

17. "Costs When Homeless and Housed in Los Angeles." Where We Sleep: Los Angeles Homeless Services Authority, 2009. 10 July 2018.

18. "Count Us In Findings." Seattle/King County Point-in-Time Count of Persons Experiencing Homelessness, Applied Survey Research, 2017, http://allhomekc.org/wp-content/uploads/2016/11/2017-Count-Us-In-PIT-Comprehensive-Report.pdf. 20 April 2018.

19. "Dealing with Unexpected Expenses." Report on the Economic Well-Being of U.S. Households in 2017, Board of Governors of the Federal Reserve System, May 2018, https://www.federalreserve.gov/publications/files/2017-report-economic-well-being-us-households-201805.pdf. 30 Aug. 2018.

20. DeAngelis, Tori. "Consumers and its discontents: Materialistic values may stem from early insecurities and are linked to lower life satisfaction, psychologists find. Accruing more wealth may provide only a partial fix." apa.org, American Psychological Association, June 2004, https://www.apa.org/monitor/jun04/discontents. 14 Jan. 2018.

21. "Disability, Employment & Homeless." nhchc.org, National Health Care for the Homeless Council, 2011, https://www.nhchc.org/wp-content/uploads/2011/09/disability2011_-final.pdf. 29 April 2019.

22. Dispositional optimism and coping: a meta-analytic review.Nes LS, Segerstrom SC. Pers Soc Psychol Rev. 2006; 10(3):235-51. 11 Aug. 2018.

23. "Domestic Violence and Homelessness: Statistics (2016)." Family & Youth Services Bureau, U.S. Department of Health & Human Services, 24 June 2016, https://www.acf.hhs.gov/fysb/resource/dv-homelessness-stats-2016. 5 April 2018

24. Durso, L.E., & Gates, G.J. (2012). Serving Our Youth: Findings from a National Survey of Service Providers Working with Lesbian, Gay, Bisexual, and Transgender Youth who are Homeless or At Risk of Becoming Homeless. Los Angeles: The Williams Institute with True Colors Fund and The Palette Fund. 13 July 2018.

25. Dworsky, Amy, et al. "Homelessness During the Transition From Foster Care to Adulthood." Am J Public Health, 2013. NCBI. 16 June 2018.

26. Edwards, Ashley. "Poverty Rate at 12.3 Percent, Down From 14.8 in 2014." census.gov, United States Census Bureau, 12 Sept. 2018.

27. "Employment and Homelessness." nationalhomeless.org, National Coalition for the Homeless, Aug. 2007, https://www.nationalhomeless.org/publications/facts/Employment.pdf. 21 Jan. 2018.

28. Ersche et al. "Abnormal Brain Structure Implicated in Stimulant Drug Addiction." science.sciencemag.org, Science, 3 Feb. 2012, http://science.sciencemag.org/content/335/6068/601.full. 1 May 2018.

29. "Estimating Unsheltered Homeless." Homeless in Sacramento County: Results from the 2017 Point-in-Time Count, California State University, Sacramento for Sacramento Steps Forward, 2017, http://www.saccounty.net/Homelessness/Documents/2017_SacPIT_Final.pdf. 4 Sept. 2018.

30. "FAQ About Homeless Veterans." National Coalition for Homeless Veterans. 10 July 2018.

31. Goodman, L., Fels, K., & Glenn, C. (2006). No safe place: Sexual assault in the lives of homeless women. Harrisburg, PA: VAWnet. 12 June 2018.

32. Guina, Ryan. "Homeless Veterans in America." themilitarywallet.com, The Military Wallet, Sept. 2018, https://themilitarywallet.com/homeless-veterans-in-america/.

33. "HIV/AIDS and Homelessness." National Coalition for the Homeless, Aug. 2007. 11 July 2018.

34. Herman, D., Susser, E., Struening, E., & Link, B. (1997). Adverse childhood experiences: Are they risk factors for adult homelessness? American Journal of Public Health, 87(2), 249-255. 10 July 2018.

35. Hodge, Charles, and Carl Castro "Combat Duty in Iraq and Afghanistan, Mental Health Problems, and Barriers to Care." The New England Journal of Medicine, 2004. 10 July 2018.

36. "Homeless Hurts: How being homeless can affect mental health." bissellcentre.org, Bissell Centre, 27 Oct. 2016, https://bissellcentre.org/blog/2016/10/27/homelessness-hurts-how-being-homeless-can-affect-mental-health/. 20 June 2018.

37. "Homeless Veterans." The 2018 Annual Homeless Assessment Report (AHAR) to Congress, The U.S. Department of Housing and Urban Development, Dec. 2018, https://www.hudexchange.info/resources/documents/2018-AHAR-Part-1.pdf. 25 April 2018.

38. "Homelessness in the United States." The 2018 Annual Homeless Assessment Report (AHAR) to Congress, The U.S. Department of Housing and Urban Development, Dec. 2018, https://www.hudexchange.info/resources/documents/2018-AHAR-Part-1.pdf. 21 Dec. 2018.

39. "How Long Does It Take to Be Approved for SSI or Social Security Disability?" Social Security Disability Resource Center, ssdrc.com. 11 July 2018.

40. "How Many People Experience Homelessness?: National Estimates of Homelessness." nationalhomeless.org, National Coalition for the Homeless, July 2009, https://www.nationalhomeless.org/factsheets/How_Many.html. 4 January 2018.

41. "HUD 2018 Continuum of Care Homeless Assistance Programs Homeless Populations and Subpopulations." CoC Homeless Populations and Subpopulations Reports, HUD Exchange, 2018, https://files.hudexchange.info/reports/published/CoC_PopSub_NatlTerrDC_2018.pdf. 21 Feb. 2018.

42. "Human Development Index." Human Development Reports, United Nations Development Programme, 2018, http://hdr.undp.org/en/composite/HDI. 7 Feb 2018.

43. Kaye, Neca, et al. "Chronic Homelessness and High Users of Health Services." National Academy for State Health Policy, 2008. 10 July 2018.

44. King County Community Services Division - Homeless and Housing Programs

45. Mae, Fannie. "Homelessness in America Americans' Perceptions, Attitudes and Knowledge." Gallup, Inc., 2007. 10 July 2018.

46. Morton, Courtney, and Ashley Williams Clark. "Homelessness, Housing in Charlotte-Mecklenburg." UNC Charlotte Urban Institute, 24 Aug. 2018.

47. National Alliance to End Homelessness. Promising strategies to end family homelessness.Washington, DC. 2006. Jun. 10 July 2018.

48. "NADAC (National Average Drug Acquisition Cost)." Medicare & Medicaid Services, 2013. Data.Medicaid.gov. 10 July 2018.

49. "New Study Offers Hope for Homeless People with Schizophrenia." endhomelessness.org, National Alliance to End Homelessness, 3 Dec. 2015, https://endhomelessness.org/new-study-offers-hope-for-homeless-people-with-schizophrenia/. 10 July 2018.

50. Nyamathi, Adeline, et al. "Risk Factors for Hepatitis C Virus Infection Among Homeless Adults." J G Intern Medicine, 2002. NCBI. 7 May 2019

51. "The Opiod Epidemic By The Numbers." Human And Health Services, 2017, hhs.gov/opioids/about-the-epidemic. 5 May 2019

52. "Overdose Death Rates." National Institute on Drug Abuse, Advancing Addiction Science, The National Institute of Health, Jan 2019, https://www.drugabuse.gov/related-topics/trends-statistics/overdose-death-rates. 17 July 2019.

53. "Population Demographics." City of Chicago 2017 Point-in-Time Count & Survey Report, Voorhees Center for Neighborhood & Community Improvement, University of Illinois at Chicago, 2017. https://www.chicago.gov/content/dam/city/depts/fss/supp_info/Homeless/2017PITSummaryReportFinal.pdf. 30 Jan 2018.

54. Philip Mangano, High Users of Publicly-Funded Health Services: A Strategy for Reducing Spending While Improving Care, (United States Interagency Council on Homelessness), presentation at Common Ground-NASHP meeting on "High Users of Publicly-Funded Health Services: A Strategy for Reducing Spending While Improving Care," held April 24-25, 2007

55. Powell, Robyn. "Can Parents Lose Custody Simply Because They Are Disabled?" American Bar Association, Apr. 2019. 5 May 2019

56. Privitera, Michael, et al. "Stress and Epilepsy." Epilepsy Foundation, 2014.

57. "Profile of Vietnam War Veterans." National Center for Veterans Analysis and Statistics, 2017. U.S. Department of Veterans Affairs. 5 May 2019

58. Rafferty, Yvonne & Shinn, Marybeth. "The Impact of Homelessness on Children: Conclusion and Social Policy Implications." semanticscholar.org, American Psychologist, Nov. 1991, https://pdfs.semanticscholar.org/5b67/873984fc0641e2d44cfb6a3a4033380fc827.pdf%5C. 9 Feb. 2018.

59. Rourke, Matt, and Alexandra Villarreal. "City Closes Encampments Filled by People Addicted to Heroin." Seattle Times, 30 May 2018.

60. Schimelpfening, Nancy. "Is There a Link Between Alcohol Use Disorder and Depression?: Co-occurrence leads to an increased risk of suicide." verywellmind.com, Verywell Mind, 5 Sept 2018, https://www.verywellmind.com/depression-and-alcohol-facts-and-statistics-1066947. 11 June 2018.

61. Siris SG. Depression in schizophrenia: perspective in the era of "atypical" antipsychotic agents. American Journal of Psychiatry 2000; 157: 1379-1389. 9 June 2018.

62. Smith, Kathleen. "Schizophrenia and Depression: Understanding The Symptoms, Risks, and Treatment Considerations." psycom.net, PsyCom, 14 Feb. 2018, https://www.psycom.net/schizophrenia-and-depression. 9 June 2018.

63. T. (2014). PART 2: Estimates of Homelessness in the United States. The 2014 Annual Homeless Assessment Report (AHAR) to Congress NOVEMBER 2015. 11 Aug. 2018.

64. "There's not a single state where a minimum wage worker can afford a 2-bedroom rental, a report says." nbc-2.com, National Low Income Housing Coalition15 June 2018. 11 Aug. 2018.

65. The link between substance abuse and posttraumatic stress disorder in women. A research review. Najavits LM, Weiss RD, Shaw SR. Am J Addict. 1997 Fall; 6(4):273-83. 11 Aug. 2018.

66. Wood, D., Harms, P., & Vazire, S. (2010). Perceiver effects as projective tests: What your perceptions of others say about you. Journal of Personality and Social Psychology, 99(1), 174-190. 11 Aug. 2018.

67. Woolley, Emma. "What are the statistics on homelessness due to divorce?" homelesshub.ca, Canadian Observatory on Homelessness/Homeless Hub: York University, 27 Feb. 2015, https://homelesshub.ca/blog/what-are-statistics-homelessness-due-divorce. 27 March 2018.